Cambridge

Elements in Politics and Society in Southeast Asia
edited by
Edward Aspinall
Australian National University
Meredith L. Weiss
University at Albany, SUNY

SINGAPORE

Identity, Brand, Power

Kenneth Paul Tan
National University of Singapore

CAMBRIDGE
UNIVERSITY PRESS

CAMBRIDGE
UNIVERSITY PRESS

University Printing House, Cambridge CB2 8BS, United Kingdom

One Liberty Plaza, 20th Floor, New York, NY 10006, USA

477 Williamstown Road, Port Melbourne, VIC 3207, Australia

314–321, 3rd Floor, Plot 3, Splendor Forum, Jasola District Centre, New Delhi – 110025, India

79 Anson Road, #06–04/06, Singapore 079906

Cambridge University Press is part of the University of Cambridge.

It furthers the University's mission by disseminating knowledge in the pursuit of education, learning, and research at the highest international levels of excellence.

www.cambridge.org
Information on this title: www.cambridge.org/9781108460460
DOI: 10.1017/9781108561273

First published 2018

A catalogue record for this publication is available from the British Library.

ISBN 978-1-108-46046-0 Paperback
ISSN 2515-2998 (online)
ISSN 2515-298X (print)

Singapore

Identity, Brand, Power

DOI: 10.1017/9781108561273
First published online: August 2018

Kenneth Paul Tan
National University of Singapore

Abstract: Contemporary Singapore is simultaneously a small postcolonial multicultural nation-state and a cosmopolitan global city. To manage fundamental contradictions, the state takes the lead in authoring the national narrative. This is partly an internal process of nation building, but it is also achieved through more commercially motivated and outward-facing efforts at nation and city branding. Both sets of processes contribute to Singapore's capacity to influence foreign affairs, if only for national self-preservation. For a small state with resource limitations, this is mainly through the exercise of smart power, or the ability to strategically combine soft and hard power resources.

Keywords: Singapore politics, society, and culture, Gramscian hegemony, Legitimacy: democracy, performance, moral authority, Multiculturalism: race, language, religion, Creative city, global city

ISBNs: 9781108460460 (PB), 9781108561273 (OC)
ISSNs: 2515-2998 (online), 2515-298X (print)

Contents

1 Singapore's Political Development through Cultural and Ideological Lenses

Since achieving independence in 1965, Singapore has today become one of the most economically prosperous countries with one of the most open economies in the world (Segarra, 2017). And yet, affluent Singapore's essentially parliamentary political system, dominated by an authoritarian state concerned fundamentally with existential matters of national survival and economic prosperity, has not evolved straightforwardly into a more competitive and expansively participatory democratic system that privileges human rights and freedoms. Modernization theory – still influential in the field of comparative politics – predicts such a transition (Inglehart and Welzel, 2009; Peerenboom, 2008; Fukuyama, 1992). American academic Christopher Lingle (1996), noting a gradual decline of electoral support for the ruling party, critiqued as unsustainable Singapore's 'authoritarian capitalism', which he described as a combination of selective economic freedoms with tough political control that rewarded loyalty and sycophancy.

Much less confident about Singapore's path to democratization and liberalization was political scientist Hussin Mutalib (2004: 28), who described Singapore as the most illiberal of democracies. He noted the ruling party's 'abhorrence of a parliamentary Opposition' and took a pessimistic view of the prospects of opposition politics. Chua Beng Huat (2017), a sociologist, argued that the Singapore government was antipathetic to western liberal democracy, grounding its hegemony on a reconstructed social democratic ideology that was present at the party's founding. Two decades earlier, Chua (1997a) had already critically examined the ruling party's efforts to produce an ideology of 'Asian communitarianism' as the basis of an anti-liberal 'Asian democracy'. Cherian George (2017), a journalist-turned-academic, wrote about and against the resilience of the Singapore government's authoritarianism, arguing in favour of political liberalization as a means of revitalizing the establishment. All three Singaporean academics – Mutalib, Chua, and George – have concluded that Singapore's political system has been and will likely continue to be resistant to democratization and political liberalization according to western, particularly US, versions.

In this Element, I note that there have been alternating cycles of political liberalization and repression, though the trend overall has been towards increasing levels of political sophistication among the establishment, the growing alternative and oppositional elites, and the electorate. I argue that Singapore's political development is better understood by paying greater attention to the ideological and cultural negotiations that occur in parallel with its material successes and failures. This is not to say that a deeply rooted political culture or ideological predisposition constrains democratic prospects in Singapore. Rather, it is the continuous work of shaping and contesting culture and ideology that creates its ever-changing and non-linear contours of political possibility. In this Element, I focus in particular on the ideological and cultural negotiations that occur in the interdependent tasks of nation building, nation and city branding, and the exercise of soft power.

It is useful to think of contemporary Singapore, for all its complexity, as having a dual nature: Singapore is simultaneously a small postcolonial multicultural nation-state and a cosmopolitan global city of the top rank. This duality has produced a dynamic variety of contradictions and tensions, which have made all the more challenging the task of keeping the authoritarian Singapore system stable, durable, and successful. For one thing, the state has had to exert continuous effort to contain, rather than resolve, these contradictions in a pragmatic (that is to say, adaptive and undogmatic) fashion whilst directing the public narration of a coherent and persuasive story that is acceptably meaningful and even inspiring to Singaporeans and other countries looking for ideas, role models, and partners for development and governance. This balancing act partly involves an internal process of nation building, but it is also achieved through more commercially motivated and outward-facing efforts at nation and city branding. Both sets of processes contribute to Singapore's capacity to influence foreign affairs, if only for national self-preservation. For a small state with resource limitations, this will mainly be through the exercise of soft (persuasive and attractive) power, which – when strategically combined with hard (military and economic) power – gives Singapore what former Harvard Kennedy School dean Joseph Nye (2013) called 'smart power'.

In this Element, I analyse the increasingly multivocal and contested nature of the Singapore narrative – undergirding its national identity, brand, and soft power – by adopting a critical-analytical approach, inspired by Antonio Gramsci, which is centred on the notion of ideological hegemony. In an advanced capitalist state like Singapore, the dominant classes assume moral leadership by forging national consensus among the diverse classes and social forces. They do this by actively and conscientiously working through their intellectuals and organic influence within civil society. Not to be confused with more straightforward notions of domination, Gramscian hegemony is an unending struggle and a dynamic 'process of creating and maintaining consensus or of co-ordinating interests' within shifting relations of domination and subordination (Slack, 1996: 144, 117–18). Developing this idea, Ernesto Laclau (1977: 161) argued that a 'class is hegemonic not so much to the extent that it is able to impose a uniform conception of the world on the rest of society, but to the extent that it can articulate different visions of the world in such a way that their potential antagonism is neutralized'. Another way to think of this is to say that hegemony is achieved in a capitalist society when common elements within discourses associated with different potentially antagonistic classes – dominant, subordinate, subaltern, etc. – are aligned.

The result of continuous struggle, negotiation, and compromise, hegemony is the basis of popular consent and political legitimacy, though it usually co-exists with other residual and emerging hegemonic formations. Hegemony is, therefore, a complex articulation that – even at its most dominant state – remains unstable and even fragile. As a conceptual tool, it is useful for analysing how consensus, achieved by connecting and containing contradictions, can just as easily be disarticulated, if pulled apart by pressures from shifting material circumstances – such as those relating to economic conditions – and their resultant changes in consciousness. Hegemony can weaken as emergent social forces forge new alliances and movements with new value systems in an ideological struggle. Thus, the maintenance of hegemony – an active process of legitimation – requires continuous ideological work, particularly as changing circumstances lead to new experiences of material disadvantage and the emergence of alternative conscious-ness. In Singapore, as Chua (1997a: 4) argued in his important work on the forging of a new consensus around an Asian communitarian ideology in the 1990s, the 'political and ideological work of the governing is, therefore, never done'.

While the Singapore state attempts continually and systematically to construct a widely acceptable ideological basis for political reasons and justifications, at the heart of which is the national narrative, its brand of authoritarianism resorts only extraordinarily – and thus rarely – to the exercise of brute force. Coercion, in the form of more overt acts of political repression, is therefore the state's last resort (Gramsci, 1971: 269), applied when ideological and cultural efforts seem to have failed. The occasional but highly tactical use of detentions without trial, lawsuits for defamation, and censorship – along with pressure applied behind the scenes – all contribute not only to a silencing of oppositional and sometimes even just alternative voices but also to a low-frequency culture of anxiety that nudges many to constrain themselves in a mode of self-censorship (Tan, 2007; Tan, 2016). George (2007) argued that most states deploy repressive tools 'rationally and with finesse' in order to consolidate authority, noting in particular the Singapore government's exercise of 'calibrated coercion' to repress its political challengers 'with minimum political cost'. This leaves the work of maintaining ideological hegemony to proceed, I argue, by drawing on at least three sources of legitimacy: the mandate arising from regular Westminster-style political elec-tions, the successful delivery of material goods, and the leadership's moral authority to rule.

In this Element, I will discuss these three ideological sources and how they relate to one another. I will then analyse how these legitimating sources are strained by the contradictions that arise from Singapore's dual nature of nation-state and global city, focussing on race, language, and religion in the nation-state and on material inequalities, creativity, and new identity politics in the global city. I will then briefly discuss how these contradictions manifest themselves in civil society, the primary location of ideological and cultural conflicts and negotiations, before examining the state's efforts to (re-)engage the citizens in national-level consultation exercises. I will then analyse how the state, driven primarily by commercial reasons and a marketing logic, produces both an inward-looking and outward-facing Singapore image, conceived as a nation/city brand that can also help to make Singapore attractive and disproportionately influential in international affairs.

2 Ideological Sources of Singapore's Hegemonic State

To gain and secure popular consent, through a basic social compact, the authoritarian state seeks to renew a strong democratic mandate through regular elections and, while in power, ensures that its extensive policies and programmes deliver results that people desire: security, wealth, social services, and a well-designed city that is liveable, for instance. Such a transactional relationship, though necessary, is not sufficient for securing lasting legimacy. Thus, the state also pays attention to the transformational dimension that gives it moral authority and an emotional appeal.

2.1 Democratic Mandate

Although Singapore displays all the formal features of a liberal democracy, having inherited the system from almost a century and a half of British colonial rule (1819–1963), what it lacks is electoral competitiveness. The ruling People's Action Party (PAP) has continued to win a significant majority of parliamentary seats since Singapore achieved self-government in 1959 (in fact, every seat in general elections fought between 1968 and 1981). This incumbency, combined with formal and informal influence over major state institutions, creative adjustments to the rules of the game (including gerrymandering), and widely recognized governmental success, has bestowed on it significant structural advantages that severely limit the prospects of opposition politics in the foreseeable future. In consequence, general elections seem unfair even though they are universal and free by international standards. The PAP publicly interprets the results of each election as a strong continuous signal of the people's mandate, countering arguments for levelling the playing field with assertions that it is 'not wise to purposely let the opposition grow bigger' (Seow, 2018). Public intellectual Ho Kwon Ping (2016), acknowledging the durability of this dominant one-party system, predicted that a transition to a two-party system might be possible only after fifteen years and likely only after thirty.

Unlike the US presidential system of governance designed to check and balance excessive power in any one organ of state, the original UK parliamentary system that Singapore inherited was designed to concentrate power in the hands of the executive, eventually in the context of a competitive two-party electoral system. Left in the postcolonial hands of Singapore, where uncompetitive elections have produced one-party parliamentary dominance since its independence, what results from regular and compulsory elections has been an enduring dominant party system with a powerful cabinet led by an even more powerful prime minister.

Since the 1980s, several constitutional changes, though often justified in seemingly 'liberal' terms, have actually made it harder for opposition parties to succeed. In 1988, for instance, the government introduced the Group Representation Constituency (GRC) system, which replaced most of the single-member constituencies. GRCs are multi-ward constituencies for which teams of parliamentary candidates, between three and six, compete during general elections. Designed principally to ensure there is minority representation in parliament, GRCs must include at least one member of parliament (MP) from a designated minority community (Malay, Indian, Eurasian, etc.). Another advantage of the GRCs – as larger administrative units – was the economies of scale they brought to the management of municipal matters. But such a change has presented opposition parties – already competing in a game with unfavourable rules – with an even more challenging task of finding good eligible candidates. In a first-past-the-post system, larger GRCs tend to reduce the electoral potency of opposition voters. GRCs also allow the PAP to field inexperienced and weaker candidates in teams anchored by more experienced ministerial incumbents, thus enabling the former to be more easily shepherded into parliament.

A second example of such constitutional changes is the introduction of an elected presidency. Since 1991, presidents – previously a merely ceremonial head of state – have been directly elected for six-year terms, during which time they cannot be members of a political party. They have the power to block the incumbent government from drawing down past reserves, approve key civil service appointments, and exercise oversight in matters relating to the Corrupt

Practices Investigation Bureau (CPIB) and the Internal Security Act.[1] While the elected presidency could seem like a liberal-inspired reform for strengthening institutional checks and balances, it can also make parliamentary opposition seem less vital from the voter's point of view. Meanwhile, the PAP government's influence over the rules of eligibility has effectively limited the electoral competition to its favoured candidates, as will be discussed later.

In the 2001 parliamentary elections, barely two months after the September 11 attacks that led to a global climate of uncertainty and an economic recession, the PAP won a historic high of 75.3 per cent of the total votes. What followed, even with the PAP's entrenched structural advantages, was a downward trend of 66.6 per cent in 2006, and then 60.1 per cent in 2011, the PAP's worst performance since independence (da Cunha, 2012; Tan, 2011). Two PAP ministers also lost their seats in 2011. In this 'new normal', many political observers expected that the PAP would lose even more votes and seats in 2015 while the opposition would raise its political profile and narrow the 'credibility gap' (Ong and Tim, 2014). It felt like modernization theory was finally exerting its inevitable pull. Instead, in the 2015 general elections, the PAP regained electoral ground, winning 69.9 per cent of the votes. It was also the first time that 100 per cent of the seats were contested. However, 2015 was also when Singaporeans grandly celebrated their fiftieth year of independence and when their first prime minister Lee Kuan Yew died. Very likely, these events had a significant pro-PAP impact on the electorate's voting behaviour.

The results, though, were still surprising given what seemed like a rising anti-establishment mood, expressed especially on social media. Many ordinary Singaporeans seemed to resent what they perceived to be the insensitivity, arrogance, self-importance, and entitled mentality of an elite and patronizing government that lacked empathy and often resorted to a defensive bullying style whenever it was confronted by even sound and constructive arguments against its reasons and decisions. Nevertheless, surveys regularly indicate that the PAP government enjoys high levels of popular trust. For instance, the 2016 Edelman Trust Barometer found that 74 per cent of Singapore's general population trusted their government, a rise of 4 per cent from 2015 (there had been a continuous decline from 2013 to 2015) (Kwa, 2016). Having only been governed by one party for all of their adult lives, most Singaporeans today can only base their decisions on a single track record, the PAP's. Since this track record basks in the glow of a state-directed national narrative featuring a heroic government

---

[1] A statute that grants the home affairs minister executive power to enforce preventive detention without trial in the interest of public order or national security.

that has transformed Singapore 'from Third World to First' in such a short period of time, the incentive for voters to risk their votes on the opposition would not seem great enough. However, the Edelman survey also noted a gap of 17 percentage points between the informed public (for whom trust levels were higher) and the mass population (for whom they were lower), which is a bigger gap than the average 12-point difference globally. Thus, if Singapore's income inequality increases further, which is not unlikely if the government continues merely to tweak their redistributive policies, there could be significant consequences for trust in the government.

Psychology professor David Chan (2017: 73–4) cautioned against 'harmful cynicism' towards political leaders that could arise when they ignore citizens' doubts and suppress their questions. These doubts and questions may legitimately come from a constructive and healthy scepticism that, he thought, should be encouraged. Instead, Chan urged leaders to turn doubt into 'conditional trust' in their competence, integrity, and benevolence, through reasonable argumentation supported by reliable evidence. While the electoral basis of the PAP government's legitimacy seems to be relatively stable, given the structural and emotional advantages that it currently enjoys, public trust in the government should not be taken for granted by an ivory-towered elite increasingly detached from the concerns and questions of the masses, as globalization brings with it greater social divisions and challenges of living a fulfilling life. The PAP government needs, as Chan would argue, to pay attention to its competence (the basis of its performance legitimacy), as well as integrity and benevolence (the basis of moral authority), both actual and perceived.

2.2 Performance Legitimacy

The PAP government formally draws its legitimacy from periodic democratic elections, but it also needs to demonstrate its ability to deliver results through efficient, effective, innovative, and far-sighted policymaking. Sometimes the two sources of legitimacy sit in tension with each other, particularly in the context of a paternalistic view that the people cannot be trusted to vote according to their long-term or 'real' interests and an undemocratic view that political opposition is merely an obstruction to the good work of the government.

Having been confronted by limited parliamentary opposition, the PAP in government has not felt so pressed to explain its every decision. Parliamentary deliberations are today televised only in the form of heavily edited clips tied to news programmes. As early as the 1970s, then politicial scientist Chan Heng

Chee (1975) already described Singapore as an 'administrative state', with a technocratic government and a depoliticized citizenry. While in government, the PAP has been able more confidently than most political parties in democratic governments to plan, formulate, and implement long-term policies well beyond the short-term political constraints of electoral cycles (Peh and Goh, 2007). Tan Gee Paw, a senior public servant who had been instrumental in driving Singapore's successful water-related policies, observed that 'in the civil service, you need to plan so far ahead that you may not even see the results in your career' (Peh and Goh, 2007). Looking for lessons from Singapore's development experience, one might argue anti-democratically that, without competitive multi-party elections, governments can lengthen their planning horizons and avoid the temptation to implement irresponsible policies aimed at making quick electoral wins at the expense of the general and long-term interest, which is usually how 'populism' is understood in Singapore. Another anti-democratic argument has been the notion that a small state like Singapore has to be nimble and act fast in order to avert a calamity or to take advantage of opportunities in a fast-changing world. Minister Teo Chee Hean (1994) once said:

> We are not playing chess where the pieces remain static while we debate and deliberate at length. We are playing football. Stop moving and the rest of the world will run rings around us . . . [L]et us not paralyse ourselves in perpetual conflict and debate.

Thus, more important than the democratic mandate has been the PAP government's performance legitimacy, particularly its capacity and proven ability to protect the people of Singapore, grow the economy, and share the nation's wealth, indirectly but palpably, with as many citizens as possible.

External security: When it comes to keeping Singaporeans safe, the PAP government's performance has been illuminated by the discourse of a small and young nation-state, vulnerable to external and internal threats (Leifer, 2000). The government officially describes its foreign policy as guided by both a set of clearly articulated principles as well as a heavy sense of realism. The government accepts that there is little it can do to change the world to suit Singapore's needs, but it can strongly support laws, rules, and norms that govern the international arena in ways that protect the sovereignty of small states like Singapore. The government maintains diplomatic relations with every country and tries to be useful and inoffensive to all, staying consistent and principled whenever it needs to advance its interest (Jayakumar, 2011). Public diplomacy and soft power are, thus, an essential component of its foreign policy arsenal. Even so, the ability to defend Singapore militarily, even for just a few weeks until help arrives, is a psychologically and politically necessary aspect of nation building. Singapore's defence budget was more than US$10 billion in 2018. In a 2016 survey, Singapore's military expenditure (between 3 and 5 per cent of its GDP each year) was the seventh-highest among countries in Asia and Oceania (Parameswaran, 2018). Singapore seems well-equipped to defend itself against military threat. And there is a well-established system of compulsory military service, which also serves as a platform for mass socialization (Huxley, 2000). Today, speaking openly about Singapore as a target of terrorism, the government has intensified its counter-terrorism capabilities and launched a comprehensive community response movement, SGSecure, to promote vigilance, cohesion, and resilience. Other external threats, the discourse around which circulates liberally in the public sphere, include cycles of economic and financial crises, spread of disease, and other non-traditional security issues, including cybercrime. Continually highlighting the severity of Singapore's external insecurity can augment the public's appreciation of its government's record of keeping Singapore safe.

Internal security: Out of a total population of 5.6 million today, Singapore has a resident population of 3.4 million Singapore citizens and 0.5 million permanent residents. The government describes Singapore society – with its resident population made up of Chinese (74.3 per cent), Malays (13.4 per cent), Indians (9.1 per cent), and 'others' (3.1 per cent) – in the rather rigid terms of a 'CMIO' model of multiracialism. There is a dualistic view in the public imagination: multiracial harmony gives cause for celebration, but racial difference also provokes anxiety. Social anthropologist Lai Ah Eng (2004) described this as a contrast between 'rituals and riots', urging Singaporeans to go beyond it. More recently, Lai (2017: 174) observed that the CMIO approach 'has been blamed for racism's prevalence and divisiveness. Deeply entrenched into government systems, it has permeated every major field and level, affecting mindsets, policy-planning, resource allocation, political representation, population profiling, public housing, educational performance and the like'.

Within the discourse of internal threats, Singapore continues to harbour collective memories of racial and religious unrest, and communist subversion, especially from the more socially and politically turbulent years of the 1950s to 1970s (Conceicao, 2007; Ramakrishna, 2015). Singapore's worst race riots in 1964, causing about 35 deaths and 560 injuries, resulted from heightened tension between the Chinese and Malays. The event is commemorated in

Singapore schools every year on 21 July when 'racial harmony day' is celebrated, and it features vividly in history textbooks that tell and re-tell The Singapore Story. Singapore's history of communist subversion is also often told in terms of the infiltration of Chinese schools and political exploitation of communal (meaning racial) issues (Singh, 2015). Part of the story also involves Singapore's sometimes troubled relationships with Malaysia and Indonesia, both imagined as giant Malay-Muslim neighbours surrounding a 'little red dot' with a Chinese majority and significant Malay-Muslim minority. Vigilance against racial and religious extremism, for instance, has made race and religion taboo subjects in the public sphere, reinforcing a siege mentality and paranoid culture that have pervaded its economic, social, and cultural life. Its narrative function is to warn Singaporeans not to take racial harmony for granted. Its ideological function is to justify the need for tough state repressive instruments such as the Internal Security Act and the Maintenance of Religious Harmony Act (designed to prevent the politicization of religion).

The CMIO model presents the government with a means of securing political legitimation by divide-and-rule; that is to say, maintaining a divided social structure that gives rise to anxiety, fear, and paranoia – the key ingredients to nourish an ideology of survival which sustains a belief that only a strong state in the form of the PAP government can protect Singaporeans from their divided selves (Kathiravelu, 2017). This culture of anxiety, nourished by a constant flow of public communications surrounding internal and external threats, amplifies the Singaporean sense of vulnerability in ways that augment the achievements of its government, justifying its extensive powers in terms of the nation's basic survival, security, and stability.

Economic growth: The government holds up economic growth as a primary, non-negotiable, and 'over-riding' goal (Chua, 1997a: 68) aimed at ensuring Singapore's survival as a vulnerable nation-state, enabling the government to finance high-quality and affordable public housing for more than 80 per cent of the population, education and health care for everyone, and infrastructure for a productive and liveable city. In the 1980s, the so-called East Asian 'tiger economies', whose successful industrial policies were yielding high economic growth rates and incomes, included Singapore, Hong Kong, South Korea, and Taiwan. In Singapore, an anxious managerial 'middle class' emerged, whose members were mostly employed by the public sector, possessed bourgeois values and aspirations, but were not motivated to press for democratization, which was what modernization theory anticipated (Jones and Brown, 1994).

This 'developmental state'[2] was able to forge peaceful industrial relations through repressive state actions, pro-business legislative amendments, the co-optation of trades unions via the National Trade Union Congress (NTUC), and a corporatist tripartite system of wage determination involving the NTUC, employers, and the government. Alongside high-quality infrastructure and attractive fiscal incentives, such arrangements, which resulted in a cheaper and more docile labour force, enabled the government to create an investment-friendly business environment that was attractive to foreign investors and MNCs, the bedrock on which Singapore's modern economy was built. Today, even as its growth rates have slowed down, Singapore is one of the richest countries in the world. Its GDP per capita grew from US$427.90 in 1960 (at current US dollars) to US$52,962.50 in 2016 (World Bank, 2018).

Sharing wealth: Policies directed at economic growth were also accompanied by policies to level up conditions for all Singaporeans so that they could live well and enjoy relatively equal opportunities to succeed, a prerequisite for social mobility and meritocracy. Rather than taking the comprehensive state welfare route, with direct handouts explicitly given to needy Singaporeans, the government instead invested extensively in public housing, education, healthcare, and urban development – including turning Singapore into a 'garden city' and now a 'city in a garden' – to elevate the mass of working-class Singaporeans to middle-class lifestyles in a fairly short space of time.

Government officials, politicians, and opinion leaders from both developing and advanced countries have acknowledged, even admired, the government's achievements in bringing about Singapore's rapid transformation. The former are keen to mimic aspects of Singapore's growth and development model, while the latter have paid much attention to its model of good governance. These desires to emulate aspects of the Singapore model have created enough of a demand for government-to-government consultancy services bearing the Singapore brand, which is also a source of its soft power.

And yet, ordinary Singaporeans – who have seen their lives improve ostensibly over the decades since independence and who keep hearing accolades for the Singapore model from overseas – have now, more than ever, become sensitive also to the government's shortcomings. Within the last couple of decades, a terrorist escaped from detention in Singapore and migrant workers rioted in Little India. Singaporeans experienced a series of flash floods,

---

[2] For more on Singapore as a developmental state, see Rodan (1989), Huff (1995), Low (2001), and Yeung (2005).

frequent train delays, and overcrowding caused by liberal immigration policies in place since the mid-2000s.

Since the late 1990s, inequality has become a significant problem. Many of the super-rich have moved to Singapore, which is now viewed not only as an Asia-Pacific centre for private banking but also as a playground for the rich and famous. Singapore is listed among the top ten cities around the world with the highest density of millionaires (Which cities around the world, 2017). While the top earners in Singapore compete for globally benchmarked salaries, the salaries of low-waged Singaporeans have been depressed by the more than a million low-waged migrant workers servicing low-productivity sectors of the economy like construction. Median incomes have generally been stagnant. Furthermore, Singapore has become one of the most expensive cities in the world. Even public housing seems much less affordable than it used to be, particularly for younger Singaporeans entering the public housing market, while the older blocks have started to see a decline in their value as they approach the end of the 99-year lease. There is doubt about whether many Singaporeans will be able to afford retirement in the near future (Bhaskaran et al., 2012). On top of all this, Singaporeans work the longest hours in the world, are the most sleep deprived, and display the highest rate of depression in Asia (Saadan, 2017; Singaporeans sleep the least, 2016; Channel NewsAsia, 2017).

A team of economists presented a paper in 2012 arguing that the alarming rise in Singapore's income inequality had resulted from an interplay of external factors such as globalization and technological developments, as well as domestic policies such as the reduction of personal income tax (which made the tax system less progressive) and liberal immigration policies (Bhaskaran et al., 2012). In other words, the government's neo-liberal policies have had a big role to play in exacerbating inequality. The government continues to view economic growth as an uncompromisable goal and neo-liberal policies as the only viable means of achieving this. Thus, it will be reluctant to go beyond tweaking the system. All the more, then, it will have to build up – in parallel with transactional modes of leadership based on material success – its ideological resources to nourish its transformational authority, motivating and inspiring the people to rally around it, usually via a call to rally around the nation (Burns, 1978). The government's moral authority is earned and maintained through continuous ideological work to contain the contradictions of the nation-state and global city.

2.3 Moral Authority

Actively contesting and then shaping Singapore's national identity, the PAP government's authoritarian politics have become institutionalized in the form of a hegemonic dominant party system. While in power for more than half a century, the PAP government has been in command of extensive political and ideological networks, resources, and instruments with which it has been able to maintain and often strengthen its hegemonic position, even, and perhaps especially, in times of economic crisis.

This elite government has been able to attract some of the most academically and professionally accomplished technocrats to join its ranks, thus strengthening its state capacity to deliver results, while justifying a highly paternalistic stance towards a mass citizenry that, in the acceptance of the comforts of affluence, have remained for the most part civically and politically infantilized. This infantilized condition shows itself clearly whenever members of the public turn helplessly, as they often do, to the authorities to solve their problems, even the most trivial ones. When members of the public disagree, instead of engaging with one another to work out these differences the almost immediate response for most has been to complain to the authorities. This pattern of behaviour relates to the 'authoritarian personality' featured in the classic work of Theodore Adorno et al. (1950). Today, government departments seem to act censoriously on behalf of every little complaint received from the public, which becomes useful as 'evidence' to support the government's often-heard argument that Singapore 'is not ready for change', particularly if the change in question challenges its authority. This aspect of its authoritarianism, a fundamentally transactional one, has very much less to do with brute force than with the apathy and contentment that pervade what George (2000) described as an 'air-conditioned nation ... of comfort and control'. But as material conditions change, as expectations rise, and as popular faith in the PAP government's competence, integrity, and benevolence weakens, the turn to a more transformational basis of authority has become more pressing.

Survival and permanent vulnerability: The government's moral authority is articulated through its public rhetoric, which has come to be quite distinctively codified. Its protective, growth, and equity functions, for instance, become all the more vital when described not as an unqualified success but as a fragile success that can easily shatter without the continued care of a capable government. From the perspective of mobilizing the people, this rhetoric of permanent vulnerability warns against complacency and gambling with the future of

Singapore. Voting for political alternatives, for instance, would be in this view an unnecessary risk that only established democracies can more easily afford. Singapore's prime minister Lee Hsien Loong readily describes his government as a 'paranoid government', always worrying about the exceptional nation's survival and future prospects. In a parliamentary speech, Lee (2007) noted how:

> Singapore's situation is totally different. We are a tiny, multi-racial, multi-religious, one little red dot out of so many red dots in the middle of Southeast Asia, lack land, lack air space, lack sea space, lack water, sometimes, also run short of sand and granite, operating in a fast-changing competitive global environment against very powerful competitors. . . . Our model is 'paranoid' government – a government which worries all the time, which plays a crucial role in this system. It is proactive and looks ahead over the horizon. Whenever people tell you not to worry, you start getting concerned.

Bilahari Kausikan (2016), a vocal retired senior diplomat, concluded a series of five public lectures with an emphatic assertion that Singapore 'will fail only if we lose our sense of vulnerability because that is what keeps us united, agile and alert'. A paranoid national rhetoric that is hyperbolic, and even at times hysterical, nourishes what Yao Souchou (2007: 28, 31, 41) described as a 'culture of excess', which constantly regenerates the experience of historical trauma and contemporary danger, manifesting itself in 'high drama', 'a sense of the tragic', 'over-responses', and an 'over-wrought imagination'. This is Singapore's ideology of survival. Alongside this is its ideology of good governance, usually comprising discourses of integrity, meritocracy, and pragmatism.

Integrity: Year after year, for several decades now, Singapore has been ranked among the least corrupt countries in the world by Germany-based Transparency International's Corruption Perceptions Index and the least corrupt country in Asia by Hong Kong-based Political and Economic Risk Consultancy (PERC). The government demonstrates its intolerance of corruption and its political will to eradicate it by dealing very severely with its own leaders and officials who have been found guilty. In fact, in the 1980s, a well-regarded minister took his own life when the government announced that he was being investigated. Such a spectacle, along with occasional reports of particular cases of high-level corruption, serves as a public ritual that reinforces the people's confidence in a government that is willing and able to serve as a check on itself, an idea that seems fundamentally at odds with western liberal democracy that seeks to limit the state's scope and capacity for abusing power by dividing its power.

Jon Quah (2003), a retired public administration professor, noted that Singapore's anti-corruption strategy has been successful because it has been able to establish, alongside its anti-corruption laws, a single specialized and independent anti-corruption agency, the Corrupt Practices Investigation Bureau (CPIB), that is reasonably well-resourced and that reports to the Prime Minister's Office (PMO) and requires the prime minister's approval to commence investigation of high-level corruption. If the prime minister were to refuse, the CPIB can turn to the separately elected president for their approval to proceed. There is a high chance of being caught for corruption. And since public sector salaries are high, the opportunity cost of corruption is also high. By streamlining and integrating bureaucratic processes and providing citizens with a simple, efficient, and electronic interface for a comprehensive range of government services, the government has not only gained administrative efficiency but also reduced opportunities for corruption. Clean and efficient government is continuously highlighted as a major factor behind Singapore's successful model of development and governance, continually nourishing the moral authority of the state. The PAP's all-white uniform visually reinforces this idea. This moral authority also strengthens the Singapore brand, which attracts importers of Singapore's management and policy expertise, investors, business people, tourists, and others who come to this global city to seek fuss-free opportunities and enjoyment.

Meritocracy: A second component of the ideology of good governance is the discourse of meritocracy. While meritocracy and democracy are not necessarily incompatible, Singapore's government usually advances an account of meritocracy, often sounding very much like a form of 'selectocracy', which runs in parallel with arguments against more electorally competitive democratic forms of governance advocated by the 'liberal west'. For this anti-democratic perspective to be compelling, the government would minimally need to find other mechanisms for ensuring that it has the best people at its disposal to do the work of leading and policymaking, that it has the right definition of 'best' (which should at the very least take into account some notion of competence, integrity, and benevolence), and that it has installed the right incentive structures to ensure that while in authority the best people are motivated to do the right things. Singapore has had a high-capacity and high-performing government, able to monopolize, through meritocratic rather than democratic institutions, the most talented Singaporeans to join the public service, particularly in leadership positions.

The PAP government is celebrated not only for its ability to design rational long-term policies but also for its ability to implement them and achieve results.

To do this, the government says it needs its most talented people to go into public service and leadership, and its rigorously meritocratic institutions – such as its education system, public sector scholarship system, Administrative Service, and some of the highest public service and political salaries in the world – have been designed to achieve this outcome. Take the scholarship system, for instance. Through a tough annual selection process, the Public Service Commission awards scholarships to study in top universities around the world. After graduation, these 'scholars' – as they are called – are employed by the public sector and 'bonded' for a designated number of years. Those who perform well are considered for the premier Administrative Service, where they are mercilessly evaluated and ranked every year. What results from these meritocratic institutions and practices is an elite government. Clean, motivated, and fairly insulated from the pressures of the local economy and society, the PAP government is able to design and implement even unpopular policies it deems to be in the long-term interest.

Singapore's discourse of meritocracy, and the public institutions and practices that are continuously narrated through it, highlights the importance of paying attention to rewarding those who are talented and qualified, who work hard, and who – through a combination of these qualities – produce results that society and the economy care for. The meritocracy discourse highlights the value of competitiveness to the degree that it motivates people, through the promise of reward, to do better than they otherwise would without such an incentive. In the context of resource scarcity, an important idea in Singapore's discourse of vulnerability, the limited pool of human talent is maximized and efficiently allocated to where it is most needed through meritocratic institutions and practices (Tan, 2008b). But these more 'capitalist' concerns are balanced by 'socialist' values such as human perfectibility and the equality of opportunity necessary for this. Indirect redistributive policies enable the worst off in society to receive the benefit of education, housing, and health, thereby increasing their potential to succeed and contribute to society, the economy, and leadership. Meritocracy, in this sense, is as much concerned about equalizing starting points as it is offering rewards that are commensurate with effort, talent, and outcome. Thus, in a properly functioning meritocracy, social mobility will ensure that all have the opportunity to do well, that those who actually do well can rise to the top, and that those at the top who no longer do well must give up their place.

Official accounts of Singapore's multiracialism intersect with this discourse of meritocracy that balances competitivenes and reward with equality of opportunity. Chinese, Malay, Indian, and other Singaporeans are said to live in a plural society where their cultural differences can flourish while individuals are treated with equality and non-discrimination by the state, which intervenes only when it views discriminatory efforts as necessary to correct or repair a structural inequality that systematically disadvantages an individual or a community. This is not always so straightforward in practice, as seen in the case of recent amendments to the Elected Presidency Act, which will be discussed later.

Pragmatism: The ability to combine 'capitalist' and 'socialist' values in meritocracy is an example of pragmatism, a third discourse in Singapore's ideology of good governance. Singapore's first prime minister, Lee Kuan Yew, described his government's pragmatism succinctly: 'If a thing works, let's work it … Our test was: Does it work? Does it bring benefits to the people?' (Lee, 1998: 109). Thus, according to this perspective, the proof of – and thus justification for – the meritocratic system is in its ability to deliver results. Outcomes outweigh principles. However, upon closer inspection, the term pragmatism has in Singapore come to mean several things over the decades, not all of which cohere neatly.

Firstly, pragmatism has meant acting in a non-dogmatic but instrumental way, eschewing any strict adherence to comprehensive moralities and ideologies on the left and right of the spectrum. Instead, the government – and only the government – has the authority to deconstruct these moralities and ideologies and to deploy their fragments as useful ideational resources that can be combined and repurposed for social, political, and even economic ends. These ends, determined by the state and impervious to popular criticism, justify the means. Hence, for instance, when it suited them, the government encouraged citizens to be rugged individuals, an American ideal, which emphasized self-reliance rather than state assistance. But at other times the government defended itself against the criticism of the liberal west by adopting useful fragments of what it imagined to be Confucian or Asian values, reconstructed and repurposed for justifying a harmonious and paternalistic system of government that was based on responsibilities more than rights, the collective over the individual, and the respect for scholarly authority ensconced in a hierarchical society. Culture has been appropriated as political-economic resource (Austin, 2001).

Secondly, the pragmatic PAP government has very little patience for philosophy, theory, or finely nuanced and elaborate arguments that circulate in academia. Lee Kuan Yew asserted that he had 'read up the theories and maybe half-believed in them. But we were sufficiently practical and pragmatic enough not to be cluttered up and inhibited by theories' (Lee, 1998: 109). What the PAP government wants is action, not talk. Ironically, this often comes down to reducing the complexity of the world into simple yes or no and right or wrong propositions, a binary point of view that betrays the acceptance of contradiction and hybridity that usually characterizes a pragmatic outlook.

The government has been willing to learn not from theory or philosophy but from best practices available anywhere in the world, believing that for every conceivable problem there is already a solution somewhere in the wider world to be studied and intelligently adapted to local circumstances. This is the third meaning of pragmatism in Singapore. Thus, public servants are regularly sent on study trips abroad to learn from others and see if what they observe may be implemented effectively.

Fourthly, while it wants to seem undogmatic, the government takes a realist perspective on human nature, accepting what it considers to be its immutable qualities. It works rationally and strategically around these qualities as parameters rather than try to transform them. Thus, if the government assumes, as it has done, that people are by nature deeply attached to their ethnic identities, then building a national identity for a multi-ethnic society must continue to acknowledge and retain ethnic categories in its essential construction. And if people are believed to be selfish and irresponsible by nature, then the government will not provide comprehensive welfare assistance for the needy because they will abuse the privilege. Rather, it will build policies around these givens – instead of seeking 'idealistically' to transform them through public education for instance – and opt for a tough principle of no free lunches. This set of realist assumptions almost dogmatically undergird the government's refusal to entertain the possibility of more explicit and extensive social welfare in a diverse multiracial society. Similarly, as discussed later, Singapore's foreign policy has also been designed around a basic realist premise that a small state cannot change the world but must navigate within its contours of power, using soft power to influence others to support rules of the game that are at the very least fair to small states. Kausikan (2016), in his public lectures, argued that a 'successful foreign policy must take the world as it is and not mistake hopes for reality', which for him was a 'cardinal sin of foreign policy'.

Fifthly, the pragmatic government has had little patience for intangible, even qualitative, values in its materialist world, unable to fully appreciate such things as metaphysical, aesthetic, sentimental, cultural, heritage, spiritual, and other aspects of life that do not readily enter into cost–benefit analysis. In the 1960s and 1970s, in the context of a heroic postcolonial modernization project, the government broadly rejected heritage conservation; but later in the 1980s – when it had been in most cases too late – the government realized its economic value, for instance where tourism was concerned, and started to take heritage more seriously (Kwek, 2004: 120). Even in the 2000s, the government continued to be somewhat indiscriminate in its destruction of the old. It tore down the much-loved National Library building, in spite of public protests, in order to build a traffic tunnel to save a few minutes of travel time. It is currently demolishing a very large number of historically significant graves in order to build a multi-lane road through a cemetery that many Singaporeans have argued should be protected. While it seems to have had little appreciation or patience for already existing cultural 'resources' for patriotism and nation-building, the government readily spends large sums of public money to manufacture national identity, sometimes through superficial campaigns and the ceremonial spectacularization of The Singapore Story.

Sixthly, the pragmatic government has, particularly since the 1990s, become more managerial in its orientation to leadership, better able to build on its techniques of organizing resources for efficient and effective outcomes, rather than engaging, inspiring, and transforming its people. In short, the government's focus has been on results and the technological and managerial techniques for achieving them ('Does it work?'), disregarding the need for adherence to comprehensive moral and ideological frameworks unless they can be repurposed to achieve desired outcomes, and disregarding in their calculations theoretical and non-material values. Without a clear and loyal sense of what traditionally fixed ideological categories of left and right mean, many Singaporeans seem relatively comfortable with ideological contradictions and hybridity as long as their favoured results are technically and managerially achieved, thus enabling the government to move in a nimble fashion, to operate in an evolutionary rather than revolutionary manner, and to more easily compromise and accommodate ideologically in order to maintain Gramscian hegemony.

The Singapore Story: A conservative national narrative that assembles as official history the founding myths and ideologies of survivalism, good governance, and their concomitent discourses of permanent vulnerability, integrity, meritocracy, and pragmatism, The Singapore Story has been the means of bridging the gap between lived experience and ideological abstraction. Historian Loh Kah Seng (1998) observed that, by the late 1970s, the PAP government started actively to construct history for ideological control, having earlier dismissed it as a regressive basis for nation building. The Singapore Story, the national narrative that gives official shape and purpose to Singapore's history, was more vigorously constructed and disseminated in the late-1990s through a 'national education' campaign ostensibly reacting to elite concerns that the younger generation did not understand or care about their national history and its leitmotif, vulnerability. This story of Singapore's founding, unlikely independence, fundamental constraints, and the PAP government's necessary role in keeping Singapore afloat, has been told and re-told in school syllabi, National Day parades and other commemorations, public speeches, television programming, and even the way that news is framed in the mainstream media. This victor's version of history entrenches the political centrality of the PAP government, with Lee Kuan Yew as the larger-than-life hero, and marginalizes – even villainizes – the PAP's opponents. The Singapore Story has been a key transformational resource for securing the PAP government's moral authority and for nation building, which have become more challenging in the context of Singapore's dual identity of nation-state and global city.

3 A Multiracial, Multilingual, and Multi-religious Nation-State

One of the foundational symbols of nationhood in Singapore is the national pledge and its daily recitation in the school system. Established in 1966, it reads: 'We, the citizens of Singapore, pledge ourselves as one united people, regardless of race, language, or religion, to build a democratic society, based on justice and equality, so as to achieve happiness, prosperity, and progress for our nation.' In urging national unity, the pledge identifies the potentially divisive quality of race, language, and religion, Singapore's traditional social cleavages.

3.1 Regardless of Race

Nation building is often thought of as 'processes that help to bridge local differences' and often also to differentiate the nation from the rest of the world (Kipnis, 2012). However, this has been much more complicated in the case of Singapore, where an unsettled form of multiculturalism that uneasily blends pluralist and integrationist approaches prevails. The pluralist approach builds upon a colonial legacy of predefined racial communities living adjacent to one another in formal equality and state-policed harmony. The integrationist approach creates and seeks to entrench a new and overarching modern postcolonial Singaporean identity, strengthened by the bridges and bonds of social cohesion, which gives every member, regardless of their position and place in the plural society, a stake in the nation (Lai, 2004). This loose blend has come to be called 'multiracialism', and it is yet another ideological resource that The Singapore Story draws upon frequently.

Sociologist Daniel Goh (2010) identified three phases of multiracialism in Singapore. The first 'melting pot' phase, from the late 1950s to 1970s, witnessed attempts by the government to socially engineer a Singaporean identity by breaking down the hard distinctions between Chinese, Malays, and Indians, replacing biological and primordial notions of racial difference, produced by colonial racial ideologies, with more culturally based – and therefore transformable – notions of ethnicity. Some of the key national institutions set up to boost this social engineering project in Singapore included public housing to give more than 80 per cent of citizens a physical stake in the country, the vast network of parastatal grassroots organizations to monitor and provide assistance to residents, mandatory military service to create a common set of 'masculine' experiences oriented towards the defence of the country, and mass cultural-national celebrations, of which the most spectacular have been the annual National Day parades.

But the founding PAP elite were quite divided on how to proceed with multiracialism and nation building. By the 1980s, Singapore entered a second phase, what Goh (2010) described as a 'mosaic' phase. Here the colonial idea of a plural society re-emerged, and racial categories – Chinese-Malays-Indians-Others – became salient again in a rigidly proportioned and simplistically constructed model that has come to be known as CMIO. To anchor this re-racialized vision of society to an evolving national identity, Singaporeans assumed hyphenated identities: Chinese-Singaporeans, Malay-Singaporeans, and Indian-Singaporeans. This has become the hegemonic notion of Singaporean national identity since then.

In 1999, then-prime minister Goh Chok Tong (1999b), alarmed by, and reacting in parliament to, nationalistic expressions emerging from a major public engagement exercise, Singapore 21, asserted in typical realist-pragmatic vein:

> I wish to caution, however, against unrealistic expectations and quick results. A strong dose of realism is necessary. A nation is not built in one generation, much less a country made up of different races and religions, who until recently, were living in different racial enclaves.

In the speech, which was titled The Singapore Tribe, Goh urged Singaporeans to think of nation and multiracialism in terms of overlapping circles: Singaporeans, especially in their private lives, were encouraged to anchor themselves to deeper cultural and moral identities related to being Chinese, Malays, Indians, or Others, while the overlapped space – constituting the public sphere – would be where a common Singaporean-ness could prevail and grow organically over time (Goh, 1999b). This model assumed that Singaporeans were naturally still 'tribally' divided, but their common national basis – though small – was sufficiently secure and would expand in its own time, with encouragement from the state.

CMIO has been the dominant model for managing ethnic diversity in Singapore, manifesting itself in the design of several policies and institutions. The 'ethnic integration policy' (EIP) was introduced in 1989 to counter the emergence of ethnic enclaves in Singapore's public housing estates by imposing ethnic quotas for each neighbourhood and each block of flats, with which buyers, sellers, and renters had to comply. Deputy prime minister Tharman Shanmugaratnam identified this 'intrusive' policy as the most important factor in explaining Singapore's success in reducing racial tension, promoting intermingling and interaction, and achieving social inclusion and stability. He argued that:

> once people lived together, they're not just walking the corridors every day, taking the same elevator up and down. Their kids go to the same kindergarten, they go to the same primary school, because all over the world, young kids go to school very near where they live. And they grow up together ... If we believe in social inclusion, if we believe in opportunities for all, we have to accept it doesn't happen automatically because of the invisible hand of the market or the invisible hand of society. It happens because you've got policies that seek to foster and encourage it.   (An investigative interview, 2015)

But the EIP has drawn criticisms too, not only for its intrusiveness. Some have argued that it is unfair to subject only public housing residents to this policy while those living in private property – the elite – are exempted from it. Also, the ethnic minority residents in public housing, who will often have a smaller pool to sell to, will generally be disadvantaged in the open market. A study has also shown that the specific impact of the policy on the behaviour of target groups has been limited (Sin, 2002).

Another set of institutions designed with CMIO in mind relates to the ethnic self-help groups (SHG), mostly in place since the 1990s. Each ethnic community has its own SHG, funded by members' monthly contributions matched by government grants. The SHGs provide financial assistance, mainly for educational support, which is tailored to the specific needs of each ethnic community. They also organize activities for cultural and community development. Of some concern has been the idea that such organizations may be effective in bonding members within ethnic groups and customizing the use of state resources for the specific needs of each community, but these are achieved at the expense of strengthening bridges across ethnic groups for the larger nation-building project. Promoting stronger identification with ethnic groups can weaken national ties and cause division.

One advantage of CMIO multiracialism is that it can keep minorities very visible and thus might prevent them from being engulfed by majoritarian interests, which seems consistent with the Singapore constitution:

(1) It shall be the responsibility of the Government constantly to care for the interests of the racial and religious minorities in Singapore. (2) The Government shall exercise its functions in such manner as to recognise the special position of the Malays, who are the indigenous people of Singapore, and accordingly it shall be the responsibility of the Government to protect, safeguard, support, foster and promote their political, educational, religious, economic, social and cultural interests and the Malay language.

In 1970, the non-elected Presidential Council for Minority Rights was set up to scrutinize most bills passed in parliament to ensure that they do not discriminate against racial and religious minority groups. Since the council hardly ever caused any bill to be amended, it might be seen as having only symbolic significance.

CMIO has also guided policy on political representation, as seen in the Group Representation Constituency (GRC) system described earlier. Up until 1991, when the constitution was amended to allow for presidents to be directly elected race-blind by the people, Singapore's presidents had been appointed by parliament to play a largely ceremonial role as head of state. Guiding their selection was an informal principle of representing each CMIO group in succession. Thus, Yusof Ishak (Malay) was president from 1965 to 1970, Benjamin Sheares (Eurasian) from 1971 to 1981, Devan Nair (Indian) from 1981 to 1985, and Wee Kim Wee (Chinese) from 1985 to 1993. In 2017, the constitution was further amended, this time to take into account CMIO multi-racialism in the elected presidency. A presidential election could be reserved for a specific racial community if, after five presidential terms, that community did not provide a president. The 'reserved' elections would be deferred to the next round if no eligible candidate from the designated community could be found. A 'community committee' has been set up to certify the candidates' race. The amendments also included a tightening of the eligibility criteria for private sector candidates who now needed to be a senior executive of a company with shareholders' equity of SG$500 million, increased from SG$100 million.

The 2017 presidential elections, a particularly illustrative example of contradictions and tensions embedded in the CMIO framework, was reserved for the Malay community. Five candidates submitted their applications. The community committee rejected two of them, both Chinese. Another two, both Malay candidates working in the private sector, failed to meet the new eligibility criterion of SG$500 million, though they would have cleared the old criterion of SG$100 million. The only eligible candidate, and thus the winner of a walkover contest in September, was Halimah Yacob. She had been speaker of parliament and a PAP MP, and thus the PAP's preferred candidate, before resigning to run for president. Halimah is also Singapore's first woman president.

CMIO multiracialism and policies that purport to protect the interests of ethnic minorities can sometimes grate against aspects of meritocracy, such as the principle of non-discrimination. According to this principle, policies should not differentiate people on the basis of their social backgrounds but should instead pay attention to the competitive results of their effort and ability. Australian political scientist Garry Rodan (2017: 4) noted that, even though many Singaporeans had in the last decade or so been sceptical of the PAP's 'ideological myth of meritocracy', they were critical of 'the compromising of meritocracy through de facto racial affirmative action'.

In the case of Halimah for president, the ideological manoeuvre to manage this contradiction between CMIO multiracialism and meritocracy has involved, firstly, making an argument against a totally colour-blind approach, since such an approach can ignore uncomfortable differences that may conceal structures of inequality preventing those from disadvantaged social backgrounds – ignored through the principle of non-discrimination – from succeeding in an intrinsically biased competition. Thus, if the Malay community seems on average to have fallen behind in postcolonial Singapore, a situation that Lily Zubaidah Rahim (1998) described as 'the persisting socio-economic marginality of the Singapore Malay community', then acting as if this were not true – in a politically correct colour-blind fashion – would be deleterious to the Malay community. With systematically fewer opportunities and resources to compete against the majority Chinese community, the starting line for Malays in Singapore is thus not equal to that for the others. The counter-argument to this is that, while the average Malay may be disadvantaged in terms of capacity and performance compared to the average Chinese and even Indian, there are also elite Malays, such as Halimah Yacob, who can compete with the best of the other racial groups. If identities are considered in an intersectional way, it will be clear that upper-middle-class Chinese, Malays, and Indians are much more similar (and comparable) to one another than they might be to their own ethnic compatriots among the working classes. Secondly, the tension between CMIO and meritocracy may be managed by arguing that someone from an ethnic minority group, even though they may be equal or better in talent and effort when compared to someone from the majority group, may still need to overcome stereotypical images of themselves (externally imposed or even deeply internalized) in order to prosper in this system. Thirdly, even if the most talented and hard-working persons from the minority group manage to overcome the negative stereotypes that distort an objective assessment of their abilities, the majority may still be inclined to prefer one of their own who may even be evidently inferior to the minority candidate.

If any of these three considerations were true, the competition would not be fair, and an argument – consistent with the principle of meritocracy – can be made for correction through policy. Such arguments, controversial as they are, have been made in support of GRCs and the reserved elected presidency, which are really 'affirmative action'-style policies. Many Singaporeans have argued in social media that Halimah – humble, well-liked, and accomplished – could have credibly won the elections on her own merits without requiring a reserved elections to protect her against a majority of Chinese voters who the government assumed would vote only for Chinese candidates. Although there was widespread use of hashtag #NotMyPresident, many argued that they were not against Halimah herself but against the new policy that robbed her of the credibility she could have earned on her own (Rodan, 2017). It may also have robbed the Malay community of their dignity. In fact, minority candidates have in the past actually won single-member constituencies against Chinese candidates without enjoying a free ride on the GRC ticket. The problem seemed overstated, and many Singaporeans were indignant about the assumption that they had not yet evolved as a nation and still behaved according to tribal loyalties.

To counter such arguments, PM Lee noted in a speech that all four candidates contesting the presidential elections in 2011 were Chinese. He asked:

> Was there a Malay candidate? ... Why didn't they come (forward)? It did not cross their minds? No ... because they knew that in an open election – all things being equal – a non-Chinese candidate would have no chance.   (quoted in S'pore's racial harmony, 2017)

Almost in support of such arguments, a backgrounder on the GRC system published in the mainstream *Today* newspaper described the system as successful in raising the proportion of minority MPs closer to the population averages:

> Between the 1988 and 2006 [general elections], the size and number of GRCs grew. By the 2006 GE, there were 14 GRCs, of which nine were five-member GRCs and five were six-member GRCs – making up 75 out of the 84 seats in Parliament. Concurrently, the number of minority MPs grew as well. Between 1988 and 2006, the number of minority MPs increased from 14 to 33, with their proportion in Parliament increasing from 16 to 27.4 per cent.   (Backgrounder, 2016)

Lee's point that Singaporeans should have 'the honesty to recognise that our multi-racialism is not yet perfect' (S'pore's racial harmony, 2017) signals perhaps an uncomfortable truth that beneath the veneer of Singapore's much-admired multiracial harmony are casual racism and day-to-day discriminatory behaviour, mainly a result of racial privilege, exercised often at an unconscious level. Popular television shows and films reveal a pattern of stereotyping that privileges the Chinese viewer while situating minority characters in roles that are unflattering, marginal, or simply non-existent (Tan, 2009). For instance, in 2017, when an Indian actor expressed outrage at being asked to exaggerate his Indian accent and mannerisms at an audition for a part in a commercial Chinese-language film, a heated debate broke out in public. Some of the sharpest criticisms had to do with the notion of Chinese privilege, theoretically derived from a more established critique of 'white privilege'. This was a critical view that Chinese Singaporeans systematically benefit from numerous advantages every day, often without even knowing it, while the non-Chinese – who are in the minority – have to work much harder to overcome obstacles that are often invisible to the majority. Even worse, to be accepted by the majority, minority citizens have to behave as if such fundamental inequalities do not exist. Naturally, the very idea of Chinese privilege is deeply offensive to many in the Chinese community who would like to be respected for their achievements, particularly for those who also struggle to survive in a highly competitive society like Singapore.

Even if the critics accepted that the problem of everyday racism, hidden privilege, and structurally disadvantaged minorities were real and should not be ignored, they may still object to the realist approach of a pragmatic government that simply accepts this as an immutable fact of Singapore society. By formulating policies around these given parameters, the policies will have the effect of perpetuating the basic problem. They might question why the government cannot try to progressively transform society through its policies and other means, such as public education, instead of reifying differences and preserving the problems by working around them.

Another type of popular criticism, rampant in social media discussions, has to do with consistency. Firstly, race is a very complicated matter that can often confound bureaucratic attempts to define it, particularly according to simplistic models like CMIO that are unable to capture the complexities of mixed-race identities, new ethnicities, and so on. Even though Halimah's father was Indian and her mother Malay, the community committee accepted her claim to being classified as Malay in this patrilineal society. Secondly, if it is argued that there must be deliberate policies to interfere with the people's choice of political leaders, in order to ensure CMIO representation, then why should this principle not also apply to the most powerful position of prime minister? Many Singaporeans – 69 per cent of 897 polled by Blackbox, for instance – have expressed enthusiastic support for DPM Tharman, an Indian, to become the next prime minister (Yong, 2016). Tharman is an impressive man, not only in terms of his public sector and political career in Singapore but also for his international accomplishments such as serving as chairman of the Group of Thirty and chairman of the G20 Eminent Persons Group on Global Financial Governance. However, the government's stand has been to say that Singapore is not ready for a non-Chinese prime minister. Critics consider these kinds of responses to be not only inconsistent with the technocratic state's claim to meritocracy (Raslan, 2016) but also hypocritical and revealing of the establishment's internal politicking.

In this regard, critics point to the CMIO multiracial justification for these constitutional changes as a fig leaf for concealing embarrassing political motivations. For instance, in the case of the reserved presidential elections, critics have noted that the hurried introduction of this change disqualified 2011 presidential candidate Tan Cheng Bock, a Chinese, from contesting. Tan had been very narrowly beaten by the PAP-supported candidate Tony Tan Keng Yam in 2011 and might have been a bigger threat to the PAP in 2017 had he been eligible to run. Rodan (2017: 5) described the elected presidency as 'one initiative where the PAP may have been too clever by half. The unintended consequences of the institution have so alarmed the PAP that it has decisively reasserted political control over the elected president process.'

As expected, there was a three-point drop in the monthly Government Satisfaction Index in September 2017, following the presidential elections walkover. Blackbox (2017), which runs this monthly public survey in Singapore, noted that there were across-the-board declines in several areas covered by this index, the highest among them being 'jobs and unemployment', 'gap between rich and poor', 'government accountability', 'civil rights', and 'cost of living'. These expressions of popular dissatisfaction, coming shortly after the presidential elections, reflect widespread frustration over the ideological contradictions surrounding race and multiracialism, which state hegemony can at best contain pragmatically through continuous ideological and cultural negotiations.

3.2 Regardless of Language

Strongly related to race, in this regard, is language. Singapore today has four official languages that resonate with the CMIO model: English, Mandarin Chinese, Malay, and Tamil. Of these four, Malay is the national language, a pidgin form of which served as the lingua franca during colonial rule. The selection of Malay as national language was made during Singapore's brief political merger with Malaysia from 1963 to 1965, and Malay retained this status even after Singapore gained Independence, though it is rarely referred to as such. Today, it is spoken by less than a fifth of the population and, at the national level, serves mainly as a ceremonial language used for military parade commands and in the national anthem *Majulah Singapura*, which roughly translates to 'Onward Singapore'.

Sociologist Nirmala Puru Shotam (1989: 503–4) observed a conjunction between language and nation in the earlier decades of independent Singapore's language policies: 'the nation would safeguard the language rights of all its citizens; while all the citizens would be responsible for answering the language demands and needs of a nation in the modern world'. With a pragmatically neutral attitude towards its colonial past, independent Singapore embraced English as the lingua franca and the language of government and administration. Since 1987, English has also been the sole medium of instruction in the national education system, which is bilingual in a very specific way: all students learn the English language (which is also the medium of instruction for nearly all their other subjects), and they also learn a second language, which is determined for them according to the race of their father, a language subject that ironically is called the 'mother tongue'. As the national education system came gradually to replace the vernacular schools (where the mediums of instruction had been the various Chinese 'dialects', Malay, and Indian languages), implementing this form of bilingualism allowed the government to demonstrate a fair and even-handed approach to the three main racial groups, using a 'neutral' and globally useful language like English to connect Singaporeans across the communities and with the larger world. By the 1980s, a hegemonic view about educational bilingualism had taken the shape of a utilitarian conception of English as the language of modernity that would give Singapore economic advantage and access to the academic, scientific, technological, business, legal, and diplomatic communities around the world; and a culturalized conception of the mother tongue as the authentic locus of expression, embedment, development, and transmission as far as culture, values, and identity were concerned (Koh, 2010).

In 2000, an annual Speak Good English Movement (SGEM) was launched in order to encourage Singaporeans to use 'standard Singapore English' instead of 'Singapore colloquial English', or Singlish, which had come to be regarded as 'broken English', a barrier to communication and understanding between Singaporeans and foreigners that the government thought would have negative economic consequences. Then-PM Goh explained that 'Poor English reflects badly on us and makes us seem less intelligent or competent', an image that he regarded as damaging to the global city's reputation and a threat to its economic edge. Singlish, according to this view, was detrimental to the Singapore brand.

Koh Tai Ann, chair of the SGEM from 2005 to 2007, argued that Singapore English, a combination of standard Singapore English and appropriately used

Singlish, was just as legitimate and effective as the mother tongue in expressing and shaping Singapore's cultural identity: 'Singlish, in easy creative co-existence with Standard English in literary works, films and drama, and used according to artistic need to reflect Singaporean life, shows that Singapore English is quite capable of effective communication and representation of the Singaporean experience and collectively, "The Singapore Story"' (Koh, 2010: 549). Many public intellectuals, arts practitioners, and upper-middle-class Singaporeans, most of whom were wholly capable of code-switching between standard English and Singlish, were of a similar view and argued against the government's denigration of Singlish.

Given the Singapore government's pragmatic orientation, all the official languages are viewed as instrumental to some larger goals, even if the mother tongue languages seem to be specially invested with culture, values, and identity. As education policy specialists S. Gopinathan et al. (2004: 232) argued, 'Language policy was essentially an instrument the state used to address issues of security, economics and culture' and was aligned with 'the economic agenda'. In the case of Mandarin, for instance, its promotion through annual 'Speak Mandarin' campaigns since 1979, the establishment of elite Special Assistance Plan (SAP) schools also in 1979 to provide students with high-level learning of Mandarin, and the nurturing of a bilingual, but also bi-cultural, Chinese elite in Singapore have much to do with economic and political purposes (Gopinathan, 2015: 47–9). At one level, it was to appease the Chinese-educated Singaporeans who felt that they were being increasingly disadvantaged in an English-speaking westernized society. At another level, it was to enable an inflow of economic benefits from the rising economic and political power of China in the world. Singapore was already positioning itself to be for the west a gateway to Asia and China.

To promote Mandarin, the government opted, with even greater vigour than it did with Singlish, to eliminate the popular use of numerous Chinese dialects such as Hokkien, Teochew, and Cantonese. The government believed that, without the distraction of dialect use, Singaporeans would become more proficient in English and Mandarin. The Chinese in Singapore would be unified under one Chinese language, and this could generate a shared Chinese culture for countering excessive westernization. The official policy to outlaw Chinese dialects has had some negative consequences. It has created a communication rift between the younger generation and their grand-parents. The pragmatic and highly instrumental approach to language has reduced the cultural richness of a diverse polyglot society. But these results have not been sufficiently harmful to enough Singaporeans in order to rally counter-hegemonic energies.

There has also been a rift within the Chinese community between those who are Chinese-educated and those who are English-educated, the former often lamenting what they see as Singapore's blind embrace of modern western values and lifestyle choices. One of the most traumatic events for the Chinese-educated was the merger of Nanyang University (Nantah) and the University of Singapore in 1980 to form the National University of Singapore. The former, the first Chinese university outside China, was officially opened in 1958, built with the money of philanthropist Tan Lark Sye as well as the contributions of a proud Chinese community that included 'wharf coolies, construction workers and dance hostesses' (Singapore Federation of Chinese Clan Associations, 1990: 31). One of the official justifications for the merger had to do with concerns about educational standards and the employability of Nantah graduates. Nantah faculty and students regarded the merger as a political attempt to assimilate the Chinese institution into the dominant English-medium university, thereby systematically marginalizing the Chinese-educated community. Some Nantah graduates have kept the 'Nantah flame' alive, resentful of what they considered to be an injustice (Ching, 1992).

On the whole, where language is concerned in Singapore, proficient speakers of English dominate. Singlish is assertively used as an expression of identity, sometimes of cultural resistance, even as the state continues to suppress it. Mandarin-speakers resent the superiority of English-speakers but enjoy dominance over speakers of still largely discouraged and devalued Chinese dialects. And Malay and Tamil speakers feel marginalized when they observe how Mandarin and English are valorized by the state. English-centred bilingualism goes some way towards moderating these social inequalities.

3.3 Regardless of Religion

While Singapore is officially described as a secular state, more than 80 per cent of Singaporeans identify with a religion. According to the 2015 census, 33.2 per cent of Singaporeans are Buddhists, 18.8 per cent are Christians, 14 per cent are Muslims, 10 per cent are Taoists and adherents of folk religions, 5 per cent are Hindus, and 18.5 per cent claim to have no religious affiliation. Religious affiliation is also intertwined with ethnicity – Chinese are mostly Buddhists and Taoists, Malays mostly Muslims, and Indians mostly Hindus. This reinforces ethno-religious lines defined by the CMIO approach (Tong, 2008). Ethno-religious identities, as encapsulated in the CMIO model, are both the objects as well as instruments of policymaking and governance in Singapore. The government's approach to secularism is not to exclude ethno-religious voices from the public realm but to police excess, encourage pro-social contributions, and harness their symbolic value for economic purposes.

The government carefully polices religious extremism, chauvinism, and fundamentalism in the interest of maintaining social order. The Internal Security Act and the Sedition Act are available for arresting those who exploit religion to threaten national security and public order. In 2001, for instance, the Internal Security Department (ISD) arrested fifteen members of Jemaah Islamiah (JI), a regional militant Islamic group, for planning to bomb embassies and other targets in Singapore, with the longer-term objective of forging a regional Islamic state. The ISD arrested another nineteen JI members the following year. In Singapore, the concern about a terrorist event, which is now envisioned in terms of 'when' rather than 'if', has as much to do with the aftermath as it does the attack itself. For instance, in the broader global context of Islamophobia, the Singapore government often worries about how Singaporeans would treat Muslims among them if their country were to be hit by a 'jihadist' attack.

Thus, the government has paid much attention to strengthening vigilance, social cohesion, and resilience, in preparation for a crisis, by building friendship and trust among the different ethno-religious groups. One state-sponsored grassroots structure for achieving this is the network of constituency-based Inter-Racial and Religious Confidence Circles (IRCCs), formed in 2002 to organize interfaith and heritage-centred activities during peacetime and to help deal with racial and religious tensions during and after a crisis. In 2003, the government issued a Declaration of Religious Harmony, to be recited by Singaporeans on Racial Harmony Day celebrated on 21 July every year. The declaration reaffirmed commitment to the secular state, social cohesion, religious freedom, respect for diversity, and inter-religious communication in a multiracial and multi-religious nation. In 2006, the government established a National Steering Committee on Racial and Religious Harmony (NSC) to be 'the national forum for apex ethnic and religious groups to dialogue and build trust across racial and religious groups in Singapore'. NSC supports the Community Engagement Programme (CEP) also launched earlier that year, following the 2005 London bombings, to 'strengthen social resilience through engagement of religious and ethnic-based organisations' (Ministry of Community Development, Youth and Sports, 2006).

The home affairs minister, through the Maintenance of Religious Harmony Act, can place restraining orders against religious leaders who cause feelings of enmity, hatred, ill will, or hostility among different religious groups; or promote political causes, carry out subversive activities, or excite disaffection against the government. But this is not to say that the government clamps down immediately on religiously affiliated people who demand that other Singaporeans, including non-religious ones, live according to their religious beliefs. In fact, the government yields to pressure from some socially conservative Christian and Muslim groups when it refuses to decriminalize homosexual acts even though more moderate Singaporeans have made arguments against such anachronistic laws that treat Singaporeans unequally. Among the influential members of the government establishment are, in fact, some who themselves hold socially conservative views informed by the Christian Right.

In the 1980s, the government treated religions as cultural resources for nation building, a realist-pragmatic approach that was willing to draw on deeper civilizational resources that were ethno-religiously based rather than build a modern synthetic national identity that did not yet have any deep foundations. Treating these traditional resources as cultural raw materials for building a national identity, instead of valuing them for their moral depth and authenticity, was, in fact, a thoroughly modern approach. In 1984, the Education Ministry introduced a new subject, religious knowledge, in secondary schools and made it a compulsory examinable subject. The intention was to provide Singaporeans in an industrialized and westernized society with moral ballasts, which could also serve as a cultural-moral bulwark against the mounting criticisms from the liberal west that centred on human rights and freedom of expression. Students could choose to study Christianity, Buddhism, Islam, Hinduism, Sikhism, or Confucianism. Even though Confucianism is not strictly speaking a religion, it was the subject on which the government placed most emphasis (Kuo, 1996: 298). To make Singapore a centre for the academic study of Confucianism, the government set up the Institute of East Asian Philosophy (IEAP), after consulting Confucian scholars from Taiwan and the United States. With its emphasis on stability, hierarchical relationships, and respect for scholars, a simplistic version of Confucianism, politically appropriated, could be ideologically useful for justifying the kind of elite authoritarian state that the PAP establishment had become by this time. Thus, the experiment in religious education was part of an ideological project to maintain state hegemony.

However, by the end of the 1980s, the government had become wary of what its Internal Security Department had reported as a rise in religious fervour. In 1987, the government used the Internal Security Act to deal with what it described as a 'Marxist conspiracy' that was linked to the Catholic Church in Singapore. By the early 1990s, religious knowledge was no longer a compulsory subject. A form of 'civil religion' replaced the use of traditional religions for nation building. In 1991, Singapore adopted a 'national ideology', which took the form of five 'shared values' that essentially enshrined the collective over the individual as well as consensus and harmony over conflict and discord. In 1992, 'civics and moral education' was introduced into the formal curriculum and then, in 1997, after publicizing survey results showing the young generation's ignorance of and disinterest in Singapore history and public affairs, the government launched the 'national education' programme that was aimed at disseminating and instilling as core values key national messages, often enacted in The Singapore Story, in all parts of the curriculum. These messages focussed on the significance of national loyalty, self-reliance, and confidence; unity in diversity; and meritocracy and incorruptibility. And then, in 2015, the idea to introduce a course on race and religion resurfaced, now aimed at preparing Singaporeans for a time of heightened religiosity, radicalism, and terrorist threats (Hetty, 2015).

Aside from its potential value as cultural resource for national identity building, Singapore's multi-religiosity has also been useful as a social resource that is able to mobilize people to volunteer to do community service and to donate towards charitable causes for the needy. Since the government has expressed an aversion to the comprehensive welfare state model, based on a realist-pragmatic assumption that people will abuse it, the socially beneficial work of churches, mosques, and temples helps to fill a gap.

The government projects Singapore's multi-religious, multilingual, and multiracial condition through the lenses of fear and of celebration, producing a formal expression of social harmony in diversity that, though fragile and potentially dangerous, provides the cosmopolitan global city with cultural resources for building social vibrancy, economic value, and a national brand, particularly where tourism, the arts, and the creative industries are concerned (Tan, 2009).

4 A Cosmopolitan Global City

Hundreds of years before British colonization, Singapore had already been a thriving port openly connected to globalized trade (Kwa, Heng, and Tan, 2009). In 1972, then foreign affairs minister S. Rajaratnam could already anticipate the broad implications of a global-city Singapore that was deeply a part of the global economic system (Heng, 2012). By the 1990s, nation-state Singapore became more profoundly embedded in the networks, flows, and dynamics of neo-liberal global capitalism. The Singapore government aimed to transform the global city into a hub of many things at the same time. Its 'global schoolhouse' concept envisioned Singapore as an education hub. Its 'renaissance city' plan outlined strategies for making Singapore a hub of the arts, media, and design. It developed strategies to become a life sciences hub and a centre for medical tourism. Singapore has become an important wealth management centre and safe haven, attracting foreign capital and individuals of high net worth through its enhanced wealth management credentials, banking secrecy laws, favourable tax arrangements, permanent residency schemes, and reputation for political stability, good governance, and a well-educated population.

All of these global hub aspirations have required the development and use of more subtle and sophisticated modes of social control to keep Singapore attractive to the profit-seeking global capitalist class deemed necessary for Singapore's own prosperity, often at the same time producing an illusion of economic, cultural, and sometimes even political liberalization. Thus, globalization has not necessarily created the conditions of authentic political liberalization for this cosmopolitan global city. Marxist geographer David Harvey, arguing that neo-liberalism is perfectly compatible with authoritarianism, characterized Singapore as having:

> combined neo-liberalism in the market place with draconian coercive and authoritarian state power while invoking moral solidarities based on ideals of a beleaguered island state (after its ejection from the Malaysian federation), of Confucian values, and most recently of a distinctive form of the cosmopolitan ethic suited to its current position in the world of international trade.   (Harvey, 2005: 86)

In the broader 'post-democratic' neo-liberal world described by sociologist Colin Crouch (2004), the rise of global capitalism coupled with a decline of progressive social forces have meant that real power is now concentrated in the hands of the political and business elite, who operate in relatively unrestrained conditions. The formal institutions of democracy, including free, fair, and competitive elections, have become spectacles of public life, substituting for serious and effective political discussion. In these post-democratic conditions, it is difficult to achieve more egalitarian and socially progressive goals. In this regard, the world's post-democracies seem to be converging on Singapore's no-longer-so-unique model.

4.1 Global City: Inequality and the Degeneration of Meritocracy

Since the mid-2000s, the government has further liberalized Singapore's already open economy, accelerating the inflow of foreigners who now make up a third of the population. Singaporeans, not generally known to be xenophobic, have started to complain about overcrowding in their city and breakdowns in their transport infrastructure, often suggesting that the immigration policy is to be blamed for this. Ironically, though, the economy has become so dependent on low-wage and low-skilled foreign workers that subsequent efforts to raise productivity and invest in technology have met with opposition from small and medium-sized local companies that argue they will be forced to go out of business or have to raise their prices, which will then raise the cost of living. For the government, restricting the infow of foreign workers and investing in productivity-raising technology can also be politically costly.

A significant number of the super-rich, such as Eduardo Severin, Nathan Tinkler, and Jim Rogers, have invested and relocated in the now-hip city. A report by property consultancy Knight Frank predicted that Singapore would see 'the world's largest influx of super-rich individuals over the next 10 years' (Lee, 2015). The attraction for them lies in Singapore's regional financial and transport hub status, its stable and pro-business government, and the large concentration of MNCs. However, the consumption patterns of the super-rich have helped to push up the cost of living, making Singapore an expensive city to live in (McDonald, 2017). As noted earlier, top earners in Singapore compete for internationally benchmarked salaries. Middle-class incomes have been stagnant even as the country rises up the ranks of the wealthiest nations. And the lowest earners experience downward pressure on their wages as they compete with nearly a million low-waged migrant workers from the region. Singapore's income inequality, as measured by the Gini coefficient, has reached highs of 0.482 in 2007 and 0.478 in 2012. UN-Habitat (quoted in Smith et al., 2015: 6) describes inequality within the 0.45 to 0.49 range as:

> approaching dangerously high levels. If no remedial actions are taken, could discourage investment and lead to sporadic protests and riots. Often denotes weak functioning of labour markets or inadequate investment in public services and lack of pro-poor social programmes.

After accounting for government transfers and taxes, however, the Gini figures are 0.439 in 2007 and 0.432 in 2012, and they do look to be declining with the cautious introduction of more progressive policies. In 2007, among OECD countries, the average post-transfers figure was 0.317, the highest was 0.480 (Chile), and the lowest was 0.240 (Slovenia). In 2012, the average was 0.316, the highest was 0.471 (Chile), and the lowest was 0.249 (Denmark) (OECD, 2016).

While the Gini coefficient might seem like just an abstract notion of income inequality subject to various statistical peculiarities, in a densely populated city like Singapore inequality is palpably experienced at the day-to-day level of the person-in-the-street. Juxtaposed uncomfortably, for instance, are images of ostentatious lifestyles of the wealthy and images of elderly Singaporeans who collect and sell discarded waste in order to make ends meet; images of luxury cars on the ever-expanding road network and images of crowded trains and irate passengers stressed out by regular breakdowns. Sociologist Teo You Yenn (2018) addressed the tensions and contradictions of highly wealthy and highly unequal Singapore through a very illuminating ethnographic presentation of the experience of low-income Singaporeans and a critical analysis of the structural and cultural conditions that reproduce inequality and poverty.

Inequality in Singapore is exacerbated periodically by globally induced economic and other forms of crises, which continue to hit globally dependent Singapore in more unpredictable and protracted ways, affecting poorer and richer Singaporeans in very different ways. Expectations of continued economic success have been moderated. With anticipated disruptions to the economy and the future of work, characterized in terms of automation and artificial intelligence, there is every likelihood that the pool of absolutely poor Singaporeans – the working poor, unemployed poor, and poor retirees who belong to an estimated 110,000 to 140,000 households (economist Yeoh Lam Keong quoted in Smith et al., 2015: xi) – will expand. For the absolutely and relatively poor households, it will be significantly harder to make ends meet, while the government maintains its restrained approach to redistributive practices, arguing that wealth generated from economic growth by the economically successful will eventually trickle down to the bottom. With Malays over-represented among poorer Singaporeans, starker inequality may reinforce the traditional social cleavages of race, religion, and language and give birth to newer ones between older and younger generations, locals and foreigners, and so on. The accelerated presence of foreigners, most of whom are in Singapore on temporary terms, has the effect of hollowing out the Singaporean core, thus weakening the sense of national and civic solidarity that needs to be the foundation of citizenship obligations and care for one another. In the near future, a highly divided society may become disenchanted, as many feel excluded from Singapore's success story for different reasons.

This future disenchantment can also be exacerbated by systematic elitism. Since the 1990s, the balance in Singapore-style meritocracy has shifted away from egalitarian values towards elitist ones. This is especially true in the way that talent is managed for political and public-sector leadership. The government started to advance arguments in the 1990s to justify a proposal to benchmark the salaries of ministers and high-ranking civil servants to the average salaries of top earners in the private sector. Significantly higher private-sector-like salaries were designed to help minimize financial 'sacrifice' and attract a future stream of talented young Singaporeans into public service, perhaps even encouraging the more entrepreneurial Singaporeans to bring their outlook and skills into the public service, which had clearly become rather technocratic following founding father Lee Kuan Yew's more heroic generation of leaders. The government also justified these salary proposals as a way of minimizing corruption, since the opportunity cost of getting caught is heightened. However, even if the realist view about people's fundamentally materialistic motivations were difficult to challenge, the multi-million-dollar salaries have remained controversial. Many Singaporeans have expressed much discomfort in the way public service motivations have now come to be equated with the 'profit motive' of the private sector. Indeed, Shamsul Haque (2004: 227–8), a professor of public administration, observed that Singapore adopted market-based reforms 'most enthusiastically' to reinvent its governance in the neo-liberal global context.

It is difficult to predict whether inequality would be a sufficient factor to bring about political change in the near future. Political scientist Meredith Weiss (2014) noted that those hardest hit by economic disloca-tion – Singapore's poorest, least adaptable, and migrants – are likely to be the least able to voice their interests through new technologies and modalities of engagement or to vote. In any case, even as online space opens up more possibilities for critical engagement that can have an effect on the outcomes of general elections, the PAP government has put in place several co-optive institutions and constitutional innovations, as discussed earlier, that severely limit the possibility of electorally unseating the PAP in the near future.

4.2 Creative City: Cosmopolitans and Heartlanders, Liberals and Conservatives

While globalization has exacerbated the problems relating to inequality and poverty in Singapore, it has also created new conditions of possibility for economic growth and development, as well as other forms of liberalization that may be seen as necessary for achieving them. As a global city with hub status in several domains, Singapore has had to upgrade its economy in many respects. In this Element, I focus on the area of creative industries, which consist of three main clusters: the arts, culture, and heritage; media and com-munications technology; and design. This is because the creative dimension relates not only to a sector of the economy but also to the broader political, social, and cultural environments needed for the next phase of economic development. It is also a primary site of cultural and ideological struggle that is ripe for critical analysis.

In 2000, the government released its first version of the Renaissance City Report. Outlining a holistic strategy that featured a significantly increased budget for supporting projects, talent development, research, infrastructure, and internationalization, the report has been its most important blueprint for the arts, culture, and heritage sectors. Similar documents have been released for the other two clusters. Since then, the value of Singapore's creative industries has risen considerably. In 2002, it was estimated to be between 2.8 and 3.2 per cent of Gross Domestic Product (GDP), lower than that of the United States (7.8), UK (5), and Australia (3.3) (Creative Industries Development Strategy, 2002). By 2009, the contribution from the three clusters had risen to 4.4 per cent of GDP, their industries employing more than 138,000 workers (Singapore Workforce Development Agency, 2015). The total nominal value-added of the arts and cultural sector alone (comprising film, cultural heritage, literary arts, performing arts, and visual arts) rose from SG$922 million in 2003 to SG$1.7 billion in 2014; its operating receipts rose from SG$5 billion to SG$7.5 billion in the same time period. The sector's workforce expanded from 23,770 in 2009 to 26,568 in 2015 (Singapore Cultural Statistics 2015, 2016). From 2003 to 2010, the number of arts companies increased by 90 per cent and arts events doubled in quantity. These numbers have generally stabilized since then.

As Singapore transitioned from its survivalist-developmental stage (1960s to 1990s) to its neo-liberal global-city stage (1990s to the present), the arts have taken three distinct trajectories that together extend into the present. These trajectories, which could be labelled 'repression', 'propaganda', and 'economic opportunity', have often been in tension with one another. The 'repression' trajectory begins with state cynicism about the arts, viewing its ability to provoke critical thinking as potentially subversive, anti-establishment, and socially destabilizing. Thus the impulse to censor work that challenges the establishment and that offends within a multiracial and multi-religious social fabric, and to arrest artists who produce such work, was really strongest during the survivalist-developmental stage. The 'economic opportunity' trajectory begins with the state's view that culture and the arts are a luxury that Singapore was not yet able to afford, since it needed to focus on satisfying Singaporeans' basic material needs and 'primary concerns' (Koh, 1989: 736). State funding mainly supported arts practices that served a propaganda func-tion – the 'propaganda' trajectory – of contributing to the performance of an evolving national narrative, the beginnings of The Singapore Story, which helped to socialize a newly industrialized, urbanized, and multiracial/multi-religious citizenry to live and work together, with modern habits of living and in rightful obedience to an authoritarian state. In the survivalist-developmental stage, Singapore appeared materialistic, uncritical, and 'culturally unsophisticated', a 'cultural desert' from which many talented artists escaped (Ho, 1964/2005: 64; Liu, 1969/2005: 21).

In the neo-liberal global-city stage, the 'economic opportunity' trajectory reached a new perspective that viewed the arts as a commercially viable sector in a knowledge-based economy. Such an economy was an upgrade on manufacturing and lower-end services, in which Singapore could no longer be cost-competitive. Jason Potts and Stuart Cunningham's (2008) work on 'competition', 'growth', and 'innovation' models of the arts helps to explain how they fit into the creative industries, which are just another potentially viable set of industries no longer in desperate need of subsidies but able also to make profits and contribute directly to economic growth. In part, this is because the creative industries also generate an atmosphere of creativity to nourish a larger ecosystem for economic development and growth. According to Potts and Cunningham (2008: 240–1), who saw this as 'part of a sustained trend in post-industrial economies', Singapore's creative industries have grown more quickly than its GDP since as early as 1986.

During this time, Singapore's arts bureaucracy started to expand. In 1988, the Ministry of Information and the Arts (MITA) was established and the government appointed an Advisory Council on Culture and the Arts, which recommended the formation of two statutory boards: the National Arts Council (NAC) was set up in 1991 and the National Heritage Board (NHB) in 1993. The Media Development Authority (MDA), the industry promoter and regulator, was formed in 2003.

In his very influential work on creative cities in the early 2000s, American economist Richard Florida (2005) found correlations among cities with high-performing economies, the presence of high-technology industries, the ability to attract very mobile global talent that made up the 'creative class', and high levels of tolerance, signalled especially by the presence of immigrants, artists, and gay people. If homophobia were viewed as the final frontier of bigotry, then cities where visibly gay people can live untroubled and harmoniously with straight people are likely to be among the most tolerant cities, where the creative and talented, whose life choices may not be so conventional, can feel safe, comfortable, and stimulated. Florida, at that time, described Singapore and a few cities in Asia (Bangkok, Osaka, Seoul, Taipei, and Tokyo) and Europe (Athens, Barcelona, Helsinki, Lisbon, Naples, and Oslo) as 'challenged by their lack of appeal to global talent'. These cities seemed to perform poorly in terms of their diversity and tolerance. Florida however acknowledged that Singapore was pursuing a strategy for improvement, highlighting its efforts to attract the top global companies and foreign talent while developing the local talent base, investing in technological infrastructure and higher education, and supporting the development of creative clusters. Singapore's strategy has also included investing heavily in artistic and cultural activity, including bolstering its Bohemian Index by supporting street-level culture. In the meantime, it has made significant strides towards becoming a more open society by openly allowing gays to work in civil-service jobs and relaxing its restrictive censorship laws. *Time* magazine had an even more optimistic view of Singapore's prospects, noting how its government would 'do "whatever it takes" to attract talent', including loosening up on 'repressive government policies previously enforced in the name of social stability' (Elegant, 2003).

Singapore's transition along the 'economic opportunity' trajectory into a creative global city has not been straightforward, brushing against the 'repression' and 'propaganda' trajectories originating in the earlier decades. In 1975 and 1976, for instance, the government launched a massive campaign under the Internal Security Act to arrest suspected communists, including Chinese theatre practitioner Kuo Pao Kun and his ballerina wife, Goh Lay Kuan. The brutality of this period and the propagandistic approach to the official performance of the national narrative for unity and cohesion have, over time, moulded an infantilized culture of fear, conformity, and censoriousness, key elements of an authoritarian personality, itself a major obstacle to Singapore becoming a vibrant creative city. In an infamous essay published in the 1990s, cyberpunk science fiction author William Gibson (1993) labelled Singapore a 'Disneyland with the death penalty'. With the 'look and feel of a very large corporation' that was 'micromanaged by a state', Singapore society seemed to him humourless, conformist, self-censoring, hardly creative, and ultimately boring. The city was a 'glassy simulacrum' revealing little of an authentic physical past. There seemed little need for policing the streets, since people policed themselves readily.

The challenge of transforming Singapore into a creative global city has also meant making the city more culturally appealing, both by loosening up cultural restraints and by designing an architecturally stimulating city with high hip factor. In this regard, Singaporeans and visitors have seen an increase in the number of theatres, concert halls, museums, and galleries. Some of the world's best restaurants are in Singapore. The iconic skyline of Marina Bay features megaprojects like Marina Bay Sands, an 'integrated resort' that includes a casino, a hotel, a convention/exhibition centre, a shopping mall, a museum, theatres, and restaurants; and the 101-hectare Gardens by the Bay, with its futuristic conservatories and 'supertrees' utilizing advanced environmental technologies. Singapore has hosted a number of major events, including the annual street-circuit night race of the Singapore Grand Prix since 2008 and the inaugural Youth Olympic Games in 2010.

Among the repressive policies that have been relaxed are those that limit artistic expression. Since 1997, busking has been allowed on the streets, but aspiring buskers must pass an audition to earn a letter of endorsement. Censorship has also been loosened up over the years, with censorship review committees convened in 1982, 1991, 2002, and 2009 to reconsider content standards and guidelines, in order to find a more appropriate balance between 'the need to protect the young, maintain social harmony and preserve general moral values'; the production of works of creative, artistic, and educational value; and increasing choice for a maturing society (Siew, 2009). The MDA's regulation strategy has shifted from censorship to industry co-regulation and consultation. But cultural liberalization, vital for supporting the creative city, has not meant relinquishing effective control over the arts and media, particularly when they are politically challenging. This, as Rodan (2004) and media scholar Terence Lee (2010) have oberved, remains key to maintaining power. In 2014, the MDA's proposal to introduce a 'self-classification' scheme for the arts was rejected by many in the arts community as a form of self-censorship, more insidious they thought than regular forms of censorship. Conservative voices also rejected the proposal for being too liberal for their comfort. Since both liberals and conservatives objected to it for opposite reasons, the proposal was aborted. This is an example of the ideological and cultural negotiations that go on continuously as the state tries to maintain its hegemony, resorting to brute force only as a last resort.

What today looks like a liberal–conservative divide in Singapore has earlier manifestations. In 1999, then-PM Goh Chok Tong (1999a) observed an emerging social divide between what he called cosmopolitans and heartlanders. The former were Singaporeans with an international outlook, whose skills and qualifications were in global demand. They could comfortably live and work anywhere in the world and command world-class salaries. Presumably, some of Singapore's cosmopolitans could have been categorized under the 'creative class' that Florida had yet to theorize then. The heartlanders, in contrast, were Singaporeans whose outlook and prospects were local. The Chinese-speaking characters in Jack Neo's commercially successful films would fit this description well. Since the late 1990s, Neo's comedic films have ideologically recruited Mandarin- and dialect-speaking audiences into an imagined marginalized community, actively othering westernized Chinese and non-Chinese Singaporeans mostly through unflattering stereotypes (Tan, 2008a). PM Goh, however, explained that both classes were potentially antagonistic, but each was vital to Singapore. For instance, cosmopolitans generated wealth for Singapore, while heartlanders preserved Singapore's core values and social stability. Goh emphasized the importance of achieving social cohesion between the two groups.

5 Civil Society and Public Engagement

In global-city Singapore, a plural society that is multiracial, multilingual, and multi-religious has become more diverse and variegated. Income and wealth inequalities, as well as the divisions between generations, heartlanders and cosmopolitans, conservatives and liberals, and locals and foreigners, have created new political challenges for the hegemonic state. A more well-educated, articulate, and digitally connected citizenry is becoming more sceptical of aspects of The Singapore Story. Public intellectuals in social media are challenging the state-influenced mainstream media, gradually shaping counter-hegemonic discourses that give recognition and voice to Singaporeans who have been left out of the Singapore success story or who have felt aggrieved by it.

The decades of a tough administrative state able to deliver results have had a depoliticizing effect on civil society. The successful state made civil society, once vibrant in the context of colonial laissez-faire (Gillis, 2005), seem irrelevant, described it as harmful, or dealt with it brutally if it effectively challenged the basis of state authority. In the late 1980s, when increasingly affluent Singaporeans became more middle-class in their lifestyle choices and value orientation, civil society re-emerged with the formation of feminist group AWARE (Association of Women for Action and Research) and race-based group AMP (Association of Malay-Muslim Professionals), as well as the revitalization of older groups like Nature Society (Singapore). The late 1980s also witnessed tough actions taken by the PAP government to control civil society, such as the arrest of twenty-two social activists for an alleged 'Marxist conspiracy' (Barr, 2010) as well as the introduction of a Maintenance of Religious Harmony Act, which outlawed the mixing of religion and politics.

In the 1990s, the government started to encourage active citizenship and 'civic' society, which it distinguished from more liberal notions of 'civil' society as a non-antagonistic, deferential, and depoliticized space to forge a sense of national togetherness, more appropriate, it argued, for an Asian society (Lee, 2002). In a landmark speech in 1991, then-arts minister George Yeo asserted:

> The problem now is that under a banyan tree very little else can grow. When state institutions are too pervasive, civic institutions cannot thrive. Therefore it is necessary to prune the banyan tree so that other plants can also grow . . . [W]e cannot do without the banyan tree. Singapore will always need a strong centre to react quickly to a changing competitive environment. We need some pluralism but not too much because too much will also destroy us. In other words, we prune judiciously.   (Yeo, 1991)

Yeo's banyan tree analogy cautiously highlighted the need for a strong state to pull back carefully, without losing its exclusive national leading role in a global environment of threats and opportunities, so that more civic institutions can emerge and function well within a society that should not be excessively diverse. However, the years following this speech witnessed yet more tough actions taken by the state to control and discipline civil society. The government placed a de facto blanket ban on specific art forms, such as forum theatre and performance art. It publicly reprimanded academics and commentators whose views it disagreed with, introducing the golfing metaphor 'out-of-bound markers' or 'OB markers' to warn Singaporeans not to cross the line (whose undefined quality naturally encouraged self-censorship). When an American academic employed at the National University of Singapore wrote an article in the *International Herald Tribune* that made unspecific references to 'intolerant regimes' in Asia that had a 'compliant judiciary', the Singapore courts took them to be a reference to Singapore, tried him and the newspaper for contempt of court, and imposed what was at the time the highest-ever fine delivered for contempt cases in Singapore.

And yet, in the late 1990s, the government started again to speak a more liberal language with respect to civil society. In a 1999 speech, then-deputy prime minister Lee Hsien Loong told his top civil servants that the government needed to 'involve and consult more people in formulating government policy' in order to 'realize the ideal of Active Citizenship'.

> Our environment in the 21st century will be very different. Our society will be more educated and sophisticated. Our problems will be more complex. We need to understand the concerns of those affected by our actions, and tap the widest range of experience and knowledge available. In a rapidly changing environment, much of the valuable and up-to-date information is held by people at the frontline. Policy makers must draw on this knowledge to understand realities on the ground, and reach better solutions. (Lee, 1999)

In a subsequent speech, Lee (2000) urged 'active citizens' to go beyond words and to take action:

> It is not enough just to express unrestrained views over drinks, or even to write critical letters to the press. If you want to have a serious influence over policy, then you must put in the effort to understand the issues, debate them knowledgeably, and have useful contributions to make. If you are not satisfied with the way things are in your own communities, then you should come forward to organise community and grassroots groups and activities, spend many evenings and weekends doing voluntary work, and patiently change things for the better.

This was followed by new policies to loosen restrictions on indoor talks and the use of Speaker's Corner for exhibitions and performances, as long as they did not involve sensitive issues, like race and religion.

In 1998, several activists and civil society organizations came together to form a loose network called The Working Committee (TWC), whose main purpose was to build social capital and help develop and nurture Singapore's civil society from the ground up (Singam et al., 2002: x). Through a series of public forums, 'open houses' held on the premises of civil society organizations, and a closing conference organized in 1999, activists and members of the public were encouraged to get to know one another, form networks, and spin off partnership projects. TWC unilaterally disbanded a year after it had been formed, as it had planned to do right from the start. By associating with one another in this loose, open, and temporary fashion, TWC did not register formally as a society and was thus able to avoid the political complications of having to do so under the Societies Act.

Today, the banyan tree remains strong and dominant. Under its shade, civil society has grown, but mostly in ways that avoid competing against the state or challenging the state openly. There are numerous private organizations (where benefits accrue to members themselves) and civic organizations (where benefits of members' efforts accrue to the larger community), but far fewer advocacy groups that try to make changes to public policy and the law by engaging with the government. Anti-death-penalty advocates for instance face an uphill challenge, as the government believes firmly that drug control requires the severest punishment. The government often ignores advocates of minimum wages or universal basic incomes who argue for more substantially redistributing the nation's wealth to achieve greater equality and well-being. The government sometimes belittles other advocates, often through ad hominem attacks, or it deals with them through subtle and behind-the-scenes methods. Today, civil society activists are mobilizing around newer causes such as heritage and history (Wang, 1998; Goh and Sim, 2012; Tan, 2015), public morality and LGBTQ issues (Chua, 2014; Chong, 2011), and immigrants and nationalism (4,000 turn up, 2013).

Meanwhile, the government continues its efforts at ideological control through national-level public engagement and envisioning exercises. When it comes to the virtues of public engagement, Singapore's clean and elite government has not been easily persuaded, in spite of the progressive rhetoric that its top leaders pronounce periodically. For most of independent Singapore's history, decisions of public importance have been taken within the administrative state's ivory tower, insulated from societal and economic pressures. Singaporeans were comfortable with strong state paternalism as long as the state was able to satisfy their material needs. The government elite often viewed citizen participation, insofar as it aligned with democratic practice, as dogmatic and an unnecessary impediment to a pragmatic means of getting results quickly and expertly.

And yet, globalization has brought greater social-cultural division and material inequalities in Singapore. Problems are more complicated and harder to solve with old formulas that used to work well. The Singapore Story of success often seems more detached from the actual lives of ordinary Singaporeans, making the nation much less easily imaginable. If this is not sensitively addressed, CMIO Singapore can splinter into old and new 'tribal' formations, creating the conditions that are ripe for social and political unrest, which would – as Gramsci theorized – invite state repression in the last resort. Thus, in spite of its authoritarian predisposition, the government acknowledged to some degree that The Singapore Story needed to be not so much re-authored but authored differently from the traditional top-down method that told a singular story from the exclusive point of view of the victors of history.

Launched by the government in August 2012, Our Singapore Conversation (OSC) was designed as a one-year series of more than 600 structured but mostly open-ended forums for about 47,000 Singaporeans (about 1 per cent of the population) to gather and discuss their aspirations for Singapore. From the start, OSC met with scepticism from the public, who doubted the authenticity of the process and the sincerity of a still-paternalistic and often condescending government. At one level, OSC was another national spectacle for taming political energies and the emerging political antagonism arising out of the problems and systemic crises inherent in Singapore's dual nature as a nation-state and global city.

However, OSC also provided a space and political opportunity that could never be fully controlled. There was space for alternative voices to persuade, negotiate, even challenge the orthodoxies of the PAP establishment. Structurally, OSC was different from earlier attempts at national-level public engagement exercises, which had been conducted since Singapore entered into the stage of neo-liberal globalization in the late 1980s. The outreach was very significantly larger than previous efforts, and so the outcomes were harder to control. The discussion agenda for OSC was relatively open-ended, and the discussions were facilitated in an inclusive rather than prescriptive way, with a much less obvious hierarchy in place.

All Singaporeans were welcome to participate and were invited to sign up for the forums, thus allowing for greater diversity of participants who engaged with one another directly. To reach senior citizens who spoke only Chinese dialects, for example, OSC organized forums in the public food centres, hosted by popular television personalities who were able to engage them in their dialects. The face-to-face discussions were also extended through social media channels, thus bringing them into a discursive space that tended to be much more cynical and confrontational. In such a context, it would have been very challenging for the government to shape the discussions in propagandistic terms, not at least without deepening the cynicism that already pervaded the public sphere.

OSC was also an occasion for building social capital, trust, and civic and democratic capabilities that the developmental state had not really invested in during the decades of rapid industrialization, when the people, focussed on being good workers and consumers, enjoyed the benefits of successful pater-nalistic government. In many ways, civic life has been impoverished by the severe imbalance of a strong and successful state and a weak citizenry. If, in contemporary Singapore, people do not adequately engage with one another and build sufficient trust, the conditions will be in place for a rapid unravelling of hegemony if material circumstances change suddenly or drastically. In spite of the government's more propagandistic intentions, public engagement exer-cises like the OSC have the incremental pedagogical potential to help both the people and the state develop their civic and democratic capabilities to engage with one another empathetically, purposefully, and effectively. Public engage-ment exercises like OSC can be a more active and potentially inclusive process of co-narrating the nation, rather than imposing a monolithic narrative of the nation on an increasingly sceptical citizenry. Thus, the tensions and contra-dictions of being a nation-state and global city would not simply be ignored but would be included in a more complex, multi-perspective, and multi-vocal narrative.

Although it continues periodically to be heavy-handed in dealing with criticism, performed perhaps as a warning to citizens against overstepping boundaries, the PAP government seems at times to be more willing to take alternative views and concerns on board, as it focusses on renewing its relation-ship with a more challenging and disenchanted electorate. Recognizing the dangers of meritocracy degenerating into crude elitism, for instance, the PAP government has made several speeches that suggest it is attempting to rebalance meritocracy, incorporating in its public rhetoric terms like 'compas-sionate meritocracy', 'inclusive meritocracy', 'meritocracy of skills not grades', and 'meritocracy through life' (for example, Tharman, 2015). Some government leaders have also spoken quite eloquently about resilience, com-plex adaptive systems, and institutionalizing diversity and debate in view of the charge that pragmatism itself seems to have narrowed into a form of dogmatism (for example, Ethos Speeches, 2009). However, the Singapore state's hegemonic success will also depend very much on whether the people see that these rhetorical manoeuvres lead to positive material changes in their lives, a challenging task for the PAP government in nation-state and global-city Singapore.

6 Nation and City Branding

Foreigners who know about Singapore, even those whose liberal sensibilities are offended by its lapses in human rights and freedom of expression, often express surprise at the way Singaporeans complain about their government, in spite of its notable material achievements. With some condescension, visitors to the country may even conclude that Singaporeans lack perspective and are ungrateful for what they have and should take a hard look at the economic, social, and political conditions in other countries that have not been as successful. Thus, in the neo-liberal global city, it is unlikely that globalization and the flows of foreigners would put political pressure on the authoritarian state to democratize.

Singapore's association with the Asian 'tiger' economies in the 1980s and its exemplary status in the eyes of the World Bank and other neo-liberal global institutions in the 1990s have sharpened its image as an economic powerhouse. Singapore also features prominently at or very near the top of global rankings on economic indicators like GDP per capita (purchasing power parity), economic competitiveness, and ease of doing business. Its airport, airline, port, and universities have been very highly ranked for many years. OECD's Programme for International Student Assessment (PISA) ranked Singapore students top in the world, not only for reading, mathematics, and science but also for their ability to work in teams to solve problems (Goh, 2017). In these respects, the Singapore brand is well regarded globally.

Today, this Singapore brand is directed at a range of external targets: investors and tourists, as well as developing countries looking at Singapore as a role model of and partner in success, and advanced countries looking to Singapore for enhancements or even alternatives to liberal democratic approaches to governance.

6.1 Nation-Branding Exercises

As Richard Florida noted in 2005, Singapore was among the Asian and European cities that lacked appeal for global talent. Its trajectories of repression and propaganda as far as culture and the arts were concerned created an image problem that was difficult to overcome. However, within the last decade, Singapore's image as a global city has vastly improved. Former journalist Koh Buck Song (2017) provided a comprehensive account of the manifold dimensions of branding Singapore, including its promotion as a liveable city with gardens, iconic skyline, glitzy mega-events, supportive business environment, legendary leaders of global stature, and the exportable know-how to make other urban locations around the world work as effectively. Koh also highlighted Singapore's achievements in the arts, including the Singapore biennale, the new National Gallery that prominently displays the canonical works of Singapore's pioneering Nanyang art movement, and local films like Boo Junfeng's *Sandcastle* and Anthony Chen's *Ilo Ilo* that have been recognized at Cannes and other major film festivals. Koh also noted sporting achievements such as Singaporean swimmer Joseph Schooling's record-breaking 2016 Olympic gold medal, Singapore's first ever, earned after beating Michael Phelps in the 100 m butterfly event. Koh highlighted Singapore's commercial brands that have made a positive contribution to brand Singapore, such as Singapore Airlines, Changi Airport, the Port of Singapore, and CapitaLand (operating in China), as well as its outward-facing non-profit volunteer and philanthropic organizations such as the Singapore International Foundation and Temasek Foundation.

Since the 1960s, the most publicly visible branding exercises for Singapore have been principally for tourism purposes. However, in a first-time joint effort in August 2017, the STB and the Economic Development Board (EDB), the pre-eminent pilot economic state agency whose main task is to attract foreign capital to invest and locate in Singapore, launched Singapore's latest global brand campaign, Passion Made Possible.

But nation branding – and state sponsorship of widespread national nostalgia – has also been a means of preserving The Singapore Story and maintaining PAP hegemony in the disruptions of a creative global city. Through a mode of nostalgia, Singaporeans are prompted to remember the past selectively, pleasurably consuming sentimentalized and romanticized versions of it that leave out inconvenient complications. In 2015, Singapore celebrated its fiftieth anniversary since independence with a high-profile series of state-sponsored projects and events, several focussing on heritage, which were branded as SG50. This was also a momentous year when Lee Kuan Yew died. Riding a wave of national pride and nostalgia, SG50 was designed to rejuvenate Singapore's national identity, strengthening a sense of belonging and community through outreach and engagement. It very likely was a major factor behind the swell of support for the PAP in its 2015 general elections, when it secured 70 per cent of the total votes.

6.2 Singapore's Model of Development and Governance

The systematization, codification, and branding of Singapore's model of development and governance became more deliberate from the 1980s, mainly as a defence against liberal criticism from the west, which intensified after the end of the Cold War. Singapore's diplomats often mounted this defence assertively. Sometimes, the west was presented as culturally and politically degenerate, with the strong implication also that it was attempting to use liberal democracy as an ideological instrument of global power. Whenever Singapore or Asia more generally were overtly challenged, the defence often involved 'occidentalizing' the west as inefficient, ineffective, corrupt, individualistic, hypocritical, and neo-imperialistic, while 'self-orientalizing' Singapore as not only an exceptional case but also an ideological alternative to liberal and human rights discourses, buoyed by Asia's rapid economic growth, rising confidence, and assertiveness. The codification of the Singapore model thus began as a defensive project rather than an exercise of introspection.

Today, there is a Singapore model, in fact a nation brand, that seems not only to have deflected many of these criticisms but also to have received positive attention and even admiration from both developing and advanced countries. The image of Lee Kuan Yew is often cast as a major part of this model and brand. His two-volume memoirs, the first of which actually bears the title *The Singapore Story*, have become essential reading for anyone looking to understand what makes Singapore tick. The books, as their opening pages indicate, have received very flattering endorsements from the most prominent political and thought leaders around the world. Another book, subtitled *Hard Truths to Keep Singapore Going* and based on interviews with Lee, was written with the purpose of educating the young generation 'on the hard truths about their country and why it needs an exceptional approach to government' (Han et al., 2011). The canon of books by Lee and on Lee has formed a kind of sacred scriptural basis for a civil religion that elevates The Singapore Story into the realm of popular piety (and, as with religious piety generally, scripture is venerated but rarely read). This can have the effect of preventing a more questioning, now seen as heretical, stance towards national history. When historian Thum Ping Tjin submitted a paper in 2018 to the Select Committee on Deliberate Online Falsehoods, in which he boldly accused Lee Kuan Yew and the PAP of defeating their political opponents in the 1960s by using a false account of their involvement in communist conspiracies, he was grilled for almost six hours, during which time the questioner focussed on discrediting his credentials and, at crucial moments, limiting his replies to yes or no answers.[3]

However, while the general public may seem particularly focussed on Lee Kuan Yew's leadership when they consider the Singapore model, as the groundswell of emotions during his funeral in 2015 might suggest, the civil service has also paid attention to the institutions and values – and not just the heroes – that have made Singapore successful. For instance, Singapore's Civil Service College has been keen 'to document the evolution in thinking and philosophy behind many important public sector initiatives over the past decade' (Ethos Speeches, 2009). Through its publications, it aims to provoke reflection – at least within the civil service – on the core values, principles, and institutions that have made Singapore successful, even as circumstances evolve.

As discussed earlier, one meaning of Singapore's pragmatism is the way that the government consciously learns and adapts best practices from anywhere in the world. And yet, PM Lee recently noted the irony of how, '[u]p to now, Singapore has had the benefit of following and adapting best practices by others who are ahead of us', but, as it moved 'closer to the leading edge', Singapore needed 'to break new ground ourselves, find fresh solutions, and feel our own way forward' (Peh and Goh, 2007). Being at the leading edge, Singapore attracts a continuous stream of overseas delegates and officials who visit to learn about its experience of rapid development to a first-world nation with a per capita GDP that ranks among the highest in the world.

Former top diplomat Kishore Mahbubani (2009) wrote about how former UK prime minister Tony Blair had told him he often met national leaders who cited Singapore as a model for their development. Opinion leaders in the west also regularly point to Singapore as an exemplar. Thomas Friedman (2011), writing in *The New York Times*, encouraged his fellow Americans to learn from Singapore and take governing seriously. Gina Rinehart, the wealthiest Australian, urged her country to look to Singapore as a model of success, reportedly saying:

> With good, responsible government, less tax, policies to welcome invest-ment and less red tape, Australia could be in Singapore's position over time ... In addition Singapore has low crime, enables guest labour, and has no debt ... Despite the country's small size, low population and lack of resources and local water supply, Singaporeans benefit significantly from its policies ... Australia is the complete opposite, despite wealth generated from vast resources.   (Pearlman, 2011)

---

[3] Full video recordings of the proceedings are available in four parts at: www.youtube.com/watch?v=7riDKnI8mO4; www.youtube.com/watch?v=ulG8smo0JVs; www.youtube.com/watch?v=F-JobEtVsQo&t=24s; and www.youtube.com/watch?v=HEFRESvJxU0.

Writing in *The Australian*, Noel Pearson (2011) urged Australian policymakers to look beyond the United States and Britain for welfare reform ideas and to see if Singapore's system of compulsory savings and universal home ownership could offer a redistributive solution through the improvement of 'the asset and wealth development capabilities of its citizens'. Conservative UK parliamentarian Owen Paterson argued, 'If we are to thrive, our post-Brexit model should exactly be Singapore, a tiny country devoid of natural resources but with a booming economy and an average life expectancy of 85' (Vasagar, 2017). *The Economist* (Go East, 2011) magazine praised Singapore's elite government, asserting that

> the place that should be learning most from Singapore is the West. For all the talk about Asian values, Singapore is a pretty Western place. Its model, such as it is, combines elements of Victorian self-reliance and American management theory. The West could take in a lot of both without sacrificing any liberty. Why not sack poor teachers or pay good civil servants more? And do Western welfare states have to be quite so buffet-like?

Singapore's social and urban policies have been especially instructive. Even in the early decades of independence, a 'clean and green' living environment was viewed as being of critical importance, not only to project a modern first-world image and to establish a good quality of life but also, as noted by a former permanent secretary of the Ministry of the Environment and Water Resources, to 'attract investments and retain talents, supporting further growth' (Tan, 2009: 5).

Singapore's public housing experience is perhaps the most impressive component of Singapore's development experience (Chua, 1997b). Through the clearance of urban kampongs and the land acquisition laws, the PAP government was able, heroically when compared to its colonial predecessor, to provide public housing for the majority of Singaporeans, today about 80 per cent of the population. The government framed a postcolonial 'housing crisis' discourse and then rapidly built sufficient housing first for victims of kampong fires such as the 1961 Bukit Ho Swee fire (framed as 'blessings in disguise') and then for the wider population housed in squatter settlements (Loh, 2013). Through the Central Provident Fund (CPF) scheme, a system of forced savings, Singaporeans could pay for their own state-subsidized public housing apartments, with a 99-year lease. Residents who owned their apartments, rather than rented them, felt more responsible for looking after their homes and their surrounding environment. Ownership gave Singaporeans a physical stake in the country and the asset value of apartments purchased in the earlier decades saw a tremendous rise, thus expanding the Singaporean 'middle class' rapidly. As described earlier, an ethnic integration policy (EIP) was introduced in 1989 to prevent ethnic enclaves from forming in the heartlands. By providing the vast majority of Singaporeans with affordable high-quality housing, the government was able to socialize them first for an industrial society and then a middle-class consumer society. The government made itself central to their daily lives and was thus able to secure political hegemony.

The government's management of Singapore's water supply is another example of innovative development policy. Historically, water has been a source of vulnerability for Singapore, which relied on long-term contracts with Malaysia for its supply. Malaysian leaders have from time to time publicly threatened to cut this supply on those occasions when relations were strained. Negotiations over the water contracts since the 1980s have also not been smooth and were often deadlocked. Since the 1970s, water-stressed Singapore has been investing heavily in water research and development; it presently has a national 'four taps' strategy, through which it is able to supplement its imported and local catchment water with water from desalination and a recycling process that produces what it calls NEWater. More than half of Singapore's water needs are today supplied through these two technologically advanced means. Water self-sufficiency, and thus a stronger hand in future negotiations with Malaysia, comes at a higher cost, and so Singapore continues to import from Malaysia for economic reasons (Lee, P. O., 2010). By pursuing a successful strategy to become a 'hydrohub', Singapore turned water from a vulnerability into a strength (Joo and Heng, 2017). Singapore positioned itself as a major research and development base for global water solutions, the demand for which is anticipated to surge in the coming decades. The National University of Singapore alone hosts an Institute of Water Policy (IWP) and a Centre for Water Research, the former focussed on water policy research and the latter on the engineering aspects of water. Since 2012, Singapore has hosted the triple-bill Singapore International Water Week, the World Cities Summit, and the CleanEnviro Summit. The Singapore hydrohub has nurtured several successful home-grown water companies, such as Hyflux and SembCorp, and a strengthening of public–private partnerships. Although these examples were profit-driven, Singapore was also motivated by altruistic purposes, playing a part in advancing the global common good by its contribution to the World Health Organization's guidelines on the quality of drinking water and its collaborations with various international organizations to host capability programmes (Joo and Heng, 2017). Since 2011, IWP has run a successful annual water leadership programme sponsored by Singapore's Temasek Foundation in collaboration with the Public Utilities Board, training hundreds of water professionals, senior engineers, consultants, and organization leaders from around the world. The Singapore hydrohub is an example of city branding that was driven along cooperative rather than competitive lines more conventionally studied in the literature (Joo and Heng, 2017).

Today, a 'Singapore franchise' markets industrial parks to China, urban solutions to India, policy education to influencers and leaders in Asia, and technical and educational products and services to the rest of the world. But Lee Kuan Yew generally held a pessimistic view, which he expressed in an interview in *The New York Times*, of other countries' capacity to copy the Singapore model, given its unique history and circumstances (Apcar, Wayne, and Mydans, 2007). Regime type, it could further be argued, determines whether the transfer of policy ideas can successfully take root and bear fruit. Singapore succeeded, as anti-democratic arguments go, because it has been led by a hegemonic dominant party state that could implement even unpopular policies it perceives to have long-term benefit without having to face strong electoral, social, and economic pressures.

From this point of view, it is hardly surprising to observe China's long-standing interest in the Singapore model. Even though China has progressed economically and socially at such a rapid pace in recent decades, it still looks for lessons from the Singapore experience and has, in fact, officially encouraged an 'upgrade' of Singapore–China relations (Zheng and Lye, 2016: xx). Zhao Lingmin (2009), a journalist in China, noted how Singapore

> remains the only country singled out by Chinese leaders for emulation. This is unprecedented in Chinese history. China has never learnt from another country so wholeheartedly for such a long period and still remained enthusiastic about it.

Public housing, eco-urbanism, and water management have been important components of Singapore's exportable township development and management expertise. In a recent study, Remi Curien (2017), a French Foreign Affairs Ministry technical advisor, noted that Singapore – with its ethnic Chinese majority and authoritarian dominant party system – is Beijing's most favoured choice as a model of modernity, urban development, and urban prestige; it has, in this regard, been a privileged partner. At the heart of the Singapore model is a city that is strictly regulated and controlled, densely organized as residential communities of tower blocks that are integrated with zones of industrial and commercial activity, and supported by technologically innovative urban infrastructure, all within a garden-like environment that is clean and green. According to Curien, the appeal of Singapore for China lies in its stable, long-term, and functionalist approach to urban planning that builds high-quality infrastructure and utilities, as well as an 'aspiration to gigantism' that motivates it to 'go big'.

The governments of Singapore and China have three joint flagship projects, which present examples of where there may be limits to the exportability of the Singapore model. The first, Suzhou Industrial Park (SIP), was established as a result of China's interest in learning Singapore's industrial development and modern management methods. Singapore's strategy in the 1990s was to regionalize its economy and take advantage of the rise of China. But the Suzhou municipal government, which had a 35 per cent stake in SIP compared to Singapore's 65 per cent, focussed instead on promoting investments in Suzhou New District (SND), a second industrial park it had built with a majority stake. SIP, with its Singapore-style 'five-star infrastructure', was charging 'five-star rents', while several low-cost industrial parks were being built nearby (Dolven, 2001). By 1999, Singapore lost about US$90 million over the first five years. It decided to take the embarrasing decision to drop its stake down to 35 per cent. Within a year of doing so, SIP started to make a profit. A report in the *Far Eastern Economic Review* concluded that the high-profile SIP debacle has 'shown the limits of Singapore as a model for economic development elsewhere'. It cited a Singaporean entrepreneur who described Singapore's loss of pride in terms of how 'our ego had been overblown when Deng Xiaoping had said in the 1980s to use Singapore as a model' (Dolven, 1999).

But the sour aftertaste did not last very long. In 2008, the Singapore government once again collaborated with the Chinese government, this time to develop Tianjin Eco-City (TEC), designed to promote social harmony, economic vibrancy, and environmental sustainability, in ways that are practicable, replicable, and scalable. Singapore does not pay for infrastructure development in TEC but instead gets experts from its agencies like the Urban Redevelopment Authority (URA), National Parks Board (NParks), National Environmental Agency (NEA), Public Utilities Board (PUB), Housing and Development Board (HDB), and Building and Construction Authority (BCA) to share their professional expertise and experience with their Chinese counterparts. The public housing development, modelled after Singapore's own experience, even includes a version of its social integration policies. In 2017, a new water reclamation centre opened in the city. A joint venture between Singapore's Keppel Infrastructure and a Chinese partner, the centre can produce 21,000 cubic metres of recycled water every day. TEC has been viewed by the Chinese government as a role model for other similar developments elsewhere. DPM Tharman, while on a visit in 2017, noted how Singapore, through TEC, could share its expertise on water management and conservation and on waterway restoration (Lim, 2017). He also outlined plans to build a park modelled after Singapore's Gardens by the Bay, turn TEC into a sensor-rich smart city, and build training infrastructure for Singapore and Chinese officials. However, in

Curien's (2017: 34) assessment, distributing the Singapore model's advantages among other cities in the rest of China faces such limitations as differences in infrastructure costs, political systems, and administrative capacity.

While the Singapore brand has been painstakingly built over the years in the interest of generating international economic opportunities and extending its soft power as a small state, it is starting to tarnish as a result of some policy failures. The frequent delays, breakdowns, and even flooding in the mass rapid transit (MRT) system in recent years may seem trivial to anyone living outside of Singapore. But in the context of state hegemony built upon faith in the government's competence, integrity, and benevolence, alongside a historical track record of delivering the goods to a very high standard, the failure to adequately provide a central public good like transportation while putting in place policies that make cars unaffordable to most ordinary Singaporeans goes right to the heart of the PAP government's legitimacy. Ordinary Singaporeans are likely to view meritocracy as now producing a well-paid elite that is aloof and insensitive to the needs of the masses, a managerial elite that focusses on the commercial aspects of public goods provision and will likely be among the few who can afford to drive in a future 'car-lite' Singapore. In the context of a densely populated global city with high cost of living and income inequality, the persistent problems with the MRT are far from trivial. An article in the *South China Morning Post* described Singapore's metro as a 'laughing stock' (Jaipragas, 2017). Veteran journalist P. N. Balji (2017) described these problems as symptoms of a 'rot that has settled into the Singapore core'.

Also drawing negative international publicity was the family dispute over Lee Kuan Yew's house on Oxley Road, where, in 1954, founding members of the PAP met regularly to discuss the establishment of the party. The legal case, surrounding Lee's wish to demolish the house after his death (regardless of its heritage value) or to keep it a closed residence for his family and their descendents, was convoluted and difficult for the public to comprehend fully. What they saw, particularly rampant on social media, was a very public feud between PM Lee Hsien Loong, who seemed to favour conserving the house, and his younger brother and sister, who seemed to want to stay faithful to Lee Kuan Yew's wish. Accusations were hurled at the PM with little restraint, alleging abuse of power, manipulation for political gain, and a betrayal of the elder Lee. Many Singaporeans, though fascinated by a voyeuristic glimpse into the private lives of the political elite, and not perhaps without a frisson of schadenfreude, nevertheless felt uncomfortable about airing Singapore's dirty linen to the world, which many considered embarrassing and inconsistent with Asian sensibilities.

Taken together, the Oxley Road house and MRT problems have prompted many to ask whether they were negative signs of things to come in a post-Lee Kuan Yew era, in which competence and high standards were no longer going to be the norm and a once-united establishment would fracture into ugly and divisive rivalry, calling into question the discourse on integrity. These more fundamental criticisms, and their nation brand implications, differed qualitatively from the 'brand keloids' that Koh (2017: location 1732, 1765) identified with such things as Singapore's chewing gum ban, nanny state behaviour, lack of media freedom, and political intolerance. Closing the deficit between the desired image and sticky negative brand perceptions such as these is much easier to do than to deal with an international perception that the Singapore model is slowly unravelling.

7 The Soft Power of a Small State

Ambassador-at-large Kausikan (2016) has argued that Singapore needs constantly to be seen as relevant in a world that does not necessarily benefit from its existence. Therefore, in Singapore, nation branding is not just about commercial gain. By outwardly showcasing all the things that 'extraordinarily successful' Singapore does well and can offer the world, such as its model of development and governance, nation branding amplifies the reasons why the world would be better off with Singapore in it. To this end, pragmatic Singapore also makes itself useful to everyone, taking a neutral stand towards global powers, refusing to take sides or show favour, except when its own sovereignty is threatened.

Kausikan finds a 'delicate balance' at the heart of Singapore's foreign policy that involves 'maintaining an omnidirectional balance in Southeast Asia by facilitating the engagement of all major powers in our region, while fostering regional cooperation through ASEAN; maintaining our economic edge and keeping our powder dry'. Its fundamental principles are spelt out clearly, even on some embassy websites:

- As a small state, Singapore has no illusions about the state of our region or the world.
- Singapore must always maintain a credible and deterrent military defence as the fundamental underpinning for an effective foreign policy;
- Singapore must promote and work for good relations with our immediate neighbours in all spheres;
- Singapore stands by its friends who have stood with it in times of need;
- Singapore is fully committed to the Association of Southeast Asian Nations (ASEAN);

- Singapore will work to maintain a secure and peaceful environment in and around Southeast Asia, especially the Asia Pacific region;
- Singapore will continue to work for the maintenance of a free and open multilateral trading system;
- Singapore is ready to trade with any state for mutual benefit and maintain an open market economy;
- Singapore will support and be active in international organisations such as the United Nations (UN).

The de facto inclusiveness of Singapore's diplomatic relations is an indicator of how successful its foreign policy has been. For instance, Arton Capital ranked Singapore's passport the most 'powerful' in the world in 2017, given the visa-free and visa-on-arrival privileges that it affords (Seow, 2017). Singaporeans thus enjoy the highest global mobility in the world. The notion of a 'powerful' passport is interesting for a small state like Singapore. Though often described as punching above its weight, Singapore views its central foreign policy problems as anchored to the fact that it is a small state, whose formal independence and sovereignty cannot guarantee that its autonomy will not actually be compromised (Kausikan, 2016).

Realist and realpolitik appoaches have been the dominant ways of understanding Singapore's foreign policy. However, Amitav Acharya (2008: 9), an international relations professor, argued that they are inadequate, pointing out that

> realism and power balancing can also be a form of 'cheap talk', a profoundly legitimizing rhetoric, easier to sell to a domestic audience which expects its leaders to be hardnosed defenders of the national interest, and to Great Power friends who do not want their patronage to be wasted on 'starry-eyed' rulers of smaller nations.

Acharya (2008: 118) noted that, in reality, Singapore's foreign policy has also been about 'socialization within regional institutions and processes' to create a 'regional existence'. As a small state, Singapore has to actively support the maintenance of and adherence to international law, institutions, and norms, which – as political scientist Ja Ian Chong (2017) argued – 'give smaller states a degree of formal equality with major powers'. Thus, the 'power' that small states like Singapore can realistically wield needs to be thought of in a different way. Joseph Nye's (2013) celebrated concept of 'soft power' is helpful in this regard.

Soft power is 'the ability to affect others to obtain preferred outcomes by the co-optive means of framing the agenda, persuasion, and positive attraction'. Nye distinguished this spectrum of behaviours from hard power, or the 'use of force and payment (and some agenda-setting based on them)'. In short, 'Hard power is push; soft power is pull'. In the case of Singapore, Kausikan (2016) – the archetypal foreign policy realist – argued that soft power 'is no substitute for hard power; you cannot have the former if you do not have the latter', which he defined mainly in terms of economic power but also the kind of military power that can produce a credible deterrent force to create stable relationships that make regional cooperation possible. In 2003, Nye (2013) had in fact coined another concept, 'smart power', or the ability to combine in various contexts hard- and soft-power resources into effective foreign policy strategies. This requires an understanding of the full range of power resources available to a country and is a much less limited approach to understanding Singapore's foreign policy options.

Among the various facets of Singapore's foreign affairs, the way this small state manages pragmatically to balance its 'special relationships' with China and with the United States is particularly illustrative of the important role played by smart power and its connection with national identity and brand. Singapore's cultural and institutional blend of east and west makes it attractive to both China and the United States, and yet it creates complications that can threaten its interests within the international order if not handled skilfully.

7.1 Singapore–USA Ties

Singapore actively supported the United States in the Vietnam War. The PAP government's anti-communist stance made Singapore ideologically and politically useful to the USA during the Cold War. But once the Cold War ended, the focus of the US government turned towards the global promotion of democracy and human rights. The liberal west has often criticized Singapore for its record on human rights, freedom of expression, freedom of assembly, and competitive elections. However, Singapore's impressive economic performance, recorded in national and international statistics, the national narrative, and the larger myth of the 'four Asian tigers', has had the effect of weakening the force and legitimacy of these liberal criticisms. As its self-confidence grew, the Singapore government expelled a Singapore-based US diplomat in 1988 for meddling in domestic politics by encouraging political opposition. In 1994, it jailed, fined, and caned an American teenager charged with vandalizing cars and stealing road signs, and this in spite of a clemency plea from US president Bill Clinton. In the 1990s, Singapore's rhetoric of Asian values was at its most strident, offered as an ideological shield against the zealous incursions of the west's liberal democratic thought and practice, reframed as a neo-colonial enterprise. By constructing an ideology first of Confucian values and later of Asian values, the Singapore government has been able not only to produce cultural explanations for its success that are different from liberal-western accounts but also to present the west as insensitive, ignorant, hypocritical, and arrogant. Today, while it continues to receive and deflect criticism from the liberal west, particularly on questions of human rights and media freedoms, Singapore presents an interesting case for considering credible alternatives to liberal democracy.

At the same time, Singapore regards USA–Singapore ties as a 'special relationship'. After China, the USA is today Singapore's second most important trading partner, and it is a major source of investment in the global city. While Singapore has stopped short of entering into a formal defence alliance with the United States in order not to provoke Malaysia and Indonesia (Acharya, 2008: 102), in 1998 Singapore and the USA formalized arrangements allowing US navy ships to berth at Singapore's Changi Naval Base. In 2012, Singapore strongly supported US president Barack Obama's 'pivot to Asia' policy, which saw the expansion of US naval power in the Asia-Pacific. Singapore also supported the Trans-Pacific Partnership (TPP), which included the United States (until it withdrew in 2018) but excluded China. In 2018, Singapore hosted a high-profile summit meeting between US president Donald Trump and North Korean leader Kim Jong-un. Presumably, Singapore was chosen because it could be relied upon for political neutrality, diplomatic professionalism, efficient event management, and laws that limit public protest. Costing the Singapore government SG$20 million, the summit generated valuable publicity for the Singapore brand and, perhaps more importantly, goodwill that can augment its soft power. The summit was also consistent with Singapore's foreign policy that, as Ja Ian Chong (2017) observed, has strongly encouraged 'comprehensive US engagement in Asia', which it has balanced with its efforts to engage China, a well-established approach of 'not choosing sides'. This assumes that US and Chinese interests overlap and each desires self-restraint and mutual accommodation.

7.2 Singapore–China ties

But 'not choosing sides' is sometimes a lot more complicated than it might seem. China is often sensitive to any indication of Singapore tilting to the United States. And the reasons for this sensitivity can be deep-seated.

The forefathers of Chinese Singaporeans mostly came from the southeastern parts of China, at first with the intention of returning to their families once their fortunes were made. Eventually, they settled in Singapore to form the majority ethnic group, but in some critical ways they absorbed the cultures of Southeast Asia (Wang, 2018). Post-1949 China was also an inspiration for progressive and socialist movements in Singapore, in which Malayan communism was able to take root before being outmanoeuvred and all but destroyed by the PAP in government. Then, in the 1970s and onwards, the pragmatic PAP government started to prepare Singapore linguistically and culturally to engage with the awakening giant, so that bilingual and bicultural Singapore could play a role in, and gain from, bridging China and the rest of the world. Indeed, Singapore – but specifically Lee Kuan Yew – did play an important role in helping the west to understand China as it opened up to the world (Zuraidah, 2017). Since the 1990s, Singapore has been collaborating with China, exporting its industrial management and urban development know-how. Today, Singapore is one of China's largest investors. However, this relationship has not been straightforward. Chinese leaders and officials persist in describing Singapore as a 'Chinese country', in spite of Singapore officials' polite protestations, and thus they expect multiracial Singapore to be deferential to China and even to take its side in, and be instrumental to, its foreign policy. Kausikan (2016) pointed out how president Xi Jinping in a 2014 speech considered overseas Chinese as 'members of the Chinese family' who shared a dream of China's rejuvenation. As China rises in global stature, poised to take over the United States as number one, both this view and this expectation have become more challenging for Singapore's foreign policy.

In 2016, under the United Nations Convention on the Law of the Sea, an international tribunal at the Permanent Court of Arbitration (PCA) at The Hague rejected China's claims to historic and other sovereign rights over territories in the South China Sea that were the subject of a long-standing dispute involving Taiwan and ASEAN countries Brunei, Malaysia, the Philippines, and Vietnam. China rejected the ruling, having refused to participate in the proceedings (Chinese social media, 2016). China expected Singapore, which had been serving as country coordinator for ASEAN–China dialogue relations, to 'respect' its rejection of the ruling and to be more supportive of China's position (Chong, 2016). Public opinion in China was also growing critical towards Singapore. Allegations were made that Singapore had failed to reciprocate China's 'brotherly affections', choosing instead to support US interests in the Asia-Pacific (China should make Singapore pay, 2016). China very likely viewed Singapore's enthusiasm for the US pivot to Asia as support for a US policy to weaken and contain China in Asia.

In his National Day rally speech that year, PM Lee reiterated Singapore's non-partisan position on the South China Sea dispute and its imperative to support a 'rules-based international order' (NDR2016, 2016). Ambassador-at-large Tommy Koh (2016) wrote an opinion piece arguing that China's view of Singapore as a 'Chinese nation' placed 'unreasonable expectations' that it would align its interests and commitments with those of China. Koh urged Singapore and China to 'try to avoid misunderstanding each other' and continue building on their history of bilateral relations. However, following its harsh criticism of Singapore's insistence on the rule of law in the South China Sea dispute, China continued to show its displeasure. In November, Hong Kong customs seized a shipment of Singapore's armoured vehicles that was en route to Singapore, transported on a commercial shipping carrier, after being routinely deployed in military exercises in Taiwan (Bland, 2016). While it seemed as if the detention was an administrative matter, there was much speculation that it was China's way of putting pressure on Singapore for its position on the South China Sea disputes and its long-time military cooperation with what Beijing regarded as a renegade province, thus failing to abide by the 'one China' policy (Chan, 2016; Seow, 2016). Later, Singapore was not invited to Beijing's inaugural Belt and Road Summit.

Although Zheng Yongnian, a Singapore-based China expert, took an optimistic view that the leaders in both countries will confidently be able to build on the bilateral ties' strong foundations laid by Lee Kuan Yew and Deng Xiao Ping (Zheng and Lim, 2016: xxvi), many Singaporeans remain concerned that relations with China would worsen and the younger generation of Singapore's political leadership could not command the same level of respect as the formidable statesman Lee Kuan Yew.

8 The Future of the Hegemonic State

Singapore's foreign affairs, in the evolving geopolitical context and the absence of Lee Kuan Yew, will become even more challenging in the coming decades. The small state's exercise of smart power and ability to deal with sharp power in the social media age must be even more compelling. Yet, the basis on which it produces soft power resources seems to be shakier as its brand, once shiny and new, starts to tarnish with age and complacency. Professional branding exercises can only go so far before the gap between image and reality stretches too wide and the external face is uncoupled from the internal fabric. Singapore's model of development and governance, systematized and codified to a high polish, cannot afford to be betrayed by too many lapses in the system and policy choices that lead to visibly adverse outcomes, such as profound socio-economic inequalities.

Once a source of dynamism and product of adaptiveness, the inherent contradictions in Singapore's institutions, practices, and rhetoric are now deepening and hardening. While neo-liberal globalization offers Singapore numerous opportunities to flourish, its institutions and practices of meritocracy and pragmatism have also started to transform more radically: the former degenerating into elitism, and the latter into an ideological fig leaf for market fundamentalism. With market fundamentalism comes greater inequalities of income and wealth, which can intersect with older cleavages of race, language, and religion, reified through an unyielding adherence to a CMIO model of society. These inequalities are exacerbated by, on one level, greater inflows of the super-rich and foreign talent to gain instant wealth and results, and, on another level, ever greater numbers of temporary migrant workers to serve as cheap labour for persistently unproductive sectors of the economy. Relative and absolute poverty, in a high-cost city with no free lunches, will become more of a problem for Singaporeans. If the government does not become more adept at meeting these challenges and provide genuine reasons for optimism, Singaporeans may turn cynical and mistrustful of the system as they observe, often through the unfiltered lenses of social media, Singapore's elite government fumble in their policymaking, shy away from technically and morally courageous policies that are necessary but risky and costly for their careers, and effect ever-greater arrogance to ward off criticism and conceal inadequacies. Ironically, Singapore's spectacular history of policy success has today routinized imagination, discouraged experimentation and bold measures, and fuelled complacency and arrogance.

But being today more profoundly embedded in globalization does of course bring more complicated problems that are harder to solve at the technical, ethical, and political levels. Policy options, demanding simultaneous attention to both the nation-state and global-city dimensions, often involve starker trade-offs, benefiting some segments of a more variegated electorate and disadvantaging many others, who are now more capable of expressing their dissatisfaction politically and electorally. Thus, performance legitimacy has become shakier grounds on which to stake the government's authority. Before too long, popular dissatisfaction may translate into electoral outcomes that will firstly weaken the PAP government, presenting it with easy populist options that – if chosen – may intensify the problems, and secondly lead to its loss of power in a dominant party system that transitions to a more competitive two-party or multi-party system. In this way, political liberalization may ultimately prevail, not as a consequence of economic growth per se and of the rise of a middle class but of the new challenges and inequities that growth presents.

In the post-Lee Kuan Yew era, will Singapore's trajectories of national identity formation, nation/city branding, and soft-power projection necessarily interact in ways that lead to ossification? Or can the PAP establishment resist political liberalization by reinventing its political regime, its political economy, and its people to become resilient in the face of future challenges? In other words, will the PAP government be able to renegotiate its hegemony by better satisfying the material needs of a people who have come to expect more from their government and by strengthening its moral authority through more compelling national narratives that modulate rather than simply assert and amplify the old ideologies of survival, fragile success, development, and governance (including discourses of integrity, meritocracy, and pragmatism)? And will the PAP government be able to achieve this before its opponents are able to consolidate the emergent counter-hegemonic ideologies against it?

It is not unrealistic to think that the PAP government can do so. For whatever weaknesess and threats have been observed looming from within and without the system, Singapore's foundations remain for the time being strong enough to support radical changes that are necessary to strengthen the regime's performance legitimacy and moral authority. These changes include, firstly, more expansive and substantive policies to redistribute resources and opportunities in an increasingly unequal and divided society. Secondly, there needs to be a move away from fear-driven, divide-and-rule governance towards greater public engagement, trust building, and inclusiveness, with a more complex appreciation of diversity. The energies of a re-emerging civil society can be constructively harnessed for this, while national public engagement exercises like Our Singapore Conversation can become even more decentralized and empowering. Thirdly, 'smart city' technology can be used not to control and stupefy the masses in a more sophisticated form of administrative infantilization but to instead facilitate collaboration; inculcate broad-mindedness, acceptance of difference, and a sense of personal responsibility; and co-imagine a Singapore global-city-nation that confidently and proudly thrives on, rather than fears, multivocality and spontaneity.

References

4,000 turn up at Speakers' Corner for population White Paper protest. (2013). *Yahoo!News*, 16 February.

Acharya, A. (2008). *Singapore's Foreign Policy: The Search for Regional Order*. Singapore: World Scientific.

Adorno, T. W., Frenkel-Brunswik, E., Levinson, D. J. & Sanford, R. N. (1950). *The Authoritarian Personality*. New York: Harper & Brothers.

An investigative interview: Singapore 50 years after independence, 45th St Gallen Symposium. (2015). www.youtube.com/watch?v=hpwPciW74b8 (1 October 2017).

Apcar, L., Wayne, A. & Mydans, S. (2007). Excerpts from an interview with Lee Kuan Yew, *The New York Times*, 29 August.

Au, A. (2009). Bloggers' maturity demonstrated in AWARE saga, *YawningBread*, April. www.yawningbread.org/arch_1998/yax-127.htm (16 January 2016).

Austin, I. (2001). *Pragmatism and Public Policy in East Asia: Origins, Adaptations and Developments*. Singapore: Fairmont International.

Backgrounder on Singapore's GRC system. (2016). *Today*, 27 January.

Barr, M. (2010). Marxists in Singapore? Lee Kuan Yew's campaign against Catholic social justice activists in the 1980s. *Critical Asian Studies*, 42(3): 335–62.

Berger, S. (2005). Singapore pushes through plan to open first casinos. *The Telegraph*, 19 April.

Bhaskaran, M., Ho, S. C., Low, D., Tan, K. S., Vadaketh, S. & Yeoh, L. K. (2012). Inequality and the need for a new social compact. Singapore Perspectives 2012 conference. Institute of Policy Studies.

Blackbox. (2017). *YouKnowAnot*, September.

Bland, B. (2016). Mystery over seized Singapore army vehicles in Hong Kong, *Financial Times*, 25 November.

Burns, J. M. (1978). *Leadership*. New York: Harper and Row.

Chan, D. (2017). *Psychological Capital: Essays by David Chan (2015–2017)*. Singapore: World Scientific.

Chan, H. C. (1975). Politics in an administrative state: where has the politics gone? In S. Meow, ed., *Trends in Singapore: Proceedings and Background Paper*, Singapore: Singapore University Press, pp. 51–68.

Chan, M. (2016). How Singapore's military vehicles became Beijing's diplomatic weapon. *South China Morning Post*, 3 December.

Channel NewsAsia (2017). Singapore's depression problem: why it matters. Television documentary.

China should make Singapore pay over South China Sea dispute, says PLA adviser. (2016). *The Straits Times*, 1 October.

Chinese social media users lash out at Singapore over S China Sea dispute. (2016). *Today*, 23 August.

Ching, C. (1992). Nanyang University alumni global reunion and the resolution of the 'Nantah Issue'. www.nandazhan.com/r1992/r92p075.htm (4 January 2006).

Chong, J. I. (2017). Singapore's foreign policy at a juncture. *East Asia Forum*, 8 November.

Chong, K. P. (2016). China asks Singapore to 'respect' its position on South China Sea ruling. *The Straits Times*, 6 August.

Chong, T., ed. (2011). *The AWARE Saga: Civil Society and Public Morality in Singapore*. Singapore: NUS Press.

Chua, B. H. (1997a). *Communitarian Ideology and Democracy in Singapore*. London: Routledge.

Chua, B. H. (1997b). *Political Legitimacy and Housing: Stakeholding in Singapore*. London: Routledge.

Chua, B. H. (2017). *Liberalism Disavowed: Communitarianism and State Capitalism in Singapore*. Ithaca: Cornell University Press.

Chua, D., Koh, J. & Yong, J. (2011). Blame it on the bogey: The Christian Right's construction of homosexuality and the AWARE CSE programme. In T. Chong, ed., *The AWARE Saga: Civil Society and Public Morality in Singapore*. Singapore: NUS Press, pp. 74–95.

Chua, L. J. (2014). *Mobilizing Gay Singapore: Rights and Resistance in an Authoritarian State*. Singapore: NUS Press.

Conceicao, J. (2007). *Singapore and the Many-Headed Monster: A New Perspective on the Riots of 1950, 1964 and 1969*. Singapore: Horizon.

Creative Industries Development Strategy. (2002) Report of the ERC Services Subcommittee Workgroup on Creative Industries, September, Singapore.

Crouch, C. (2004). *Post-Democracy*. Cambridge, UK: Polity.

Curien, R. (2017). Singapore, a model for (sustainable?) urban development in China: an overview of 20 years of Sino-Singaporean cooperation, *China Perspectives*, 1: 25–35.

da Cunha, D. (2010). *Singapore Places Its Bets: Casinos, Foreign Talent, and Remaking a City-State*. Singapore: Straits Times Press.

da Cunha, D. (2012). *Breakthrough: Roadmap for Singapore's Political Future*. Singapore: Straits Times Press.

Department of Statistics Singapore. (2017). *Population Trends 2017*. Singapore.

Dolven, B. (1999). Suzhou project: wounded pride. *Far Eastern Economic Review*, 8 July.

Dolven, B. (2001). The new frontier. *Far Eastern Economic Review*, 6 December.

Elegant, S. (2003). A lion in winter. *Time*, 30 June.

Ethos Speeches: In Time For The Future: Singapore's Heads of Civil Service on Change, Complexity and Networked Government. (2009). Singapore: Civil Service College.

Florida, R. (2005). *The Flight of the Creative Class: The New Global Competition for Talent.* New York: HarperCollins.

Friedman, T. (2011). Serious in Singapore. *The New York Times*, 29 January.

Fukuyama, F. (1992). *The End of History and the Last Man.* London: Hamish Hamilton.

George, C. (2000). *Singapore: The Air-Conditioned Nation: Essays on the Politics of Comfort and Control 1990–2000.* Singapore: Landmark.

George, C. (2007). Consolidating authoritarian rule: calibrated coercion in Singapore. *The Pacific Review*, 20(2): 127–45.

George, C. (2017). *Singapore, Incomplete: Reflections on a First World Nation's Arrested Political Development.* Singapore: Ethos.

George, T. J. S. (1973). *Lee Kuan Yew's Singapore.* London: Deutsch.

Gibson, W. (1993). Disneyland with the death penalty. *Wired*, 1(04). www .wired.com/wired/archive/1.04/gibson_pr.html (29 January 2016).

Gillis, E. K. (2005). *Singapore Civil Society and British Power.* Singapore: Talisman.

Go East, young bureaucrat. (2011). *The Economist*, 17 May.

Goh, C. (2017). Singapore students are best team players: PISA study. *Channel NewsAsia*, 21 November.

Goh, C. L. & Sim, R. (2012). Bukit Brown meeting 'not a consultation'. *The Straits Times*, 21 March.

Goh, C. T. (1999a). National Day Rally speech. 22 August, Singapore.

Goh, C. T. (1999b). The Singapore tribe, speech by Prime Minister Goh Chok Tong on the Singapore 21 Debate in Parliament, 5 May.

Goh, P. S. D. (2010). Multiculturalism and the problem of solidarity. In T. Chong, ed., *Management of Success: Singapore Revisited.* Singapore: ISEAS, pp. 561–78.

Goh, P. S. D., Gabrielpillai, M. & Holden, P. eds. (2009). *Race and Multiculturalism in Malaysia and Singapore.* London: Routledge.

Gopinathan, S. (2015). *Education.* Singapore: Straits Times Press.

Gopinathan, S., Ho, W.K. & Saravanan, V. (2004). Ethnicity management and language education policy: Towards a modified model of language education in Singapore schools. In Lai, A. E., ed., *Beyond Rituals and Riots: Ethnic Pluralism and Social Cohesion in Singapore*. Singapore: Eastern Universities Press.

Gramsci, A. (ed. and trans. Q. Hoare and G.N. Smith). (1971). *Selections from the Prison Notebooks*. New York: International Publishers.

Han, F. K. (2009). How ST covered the story. *The Straits Times*, 30 May.

Han, F. K. et al. (2011). *Lee Kuan Yew: Hard Truths to Keep Singapore Going*. Singapore: Straits Times Press.

Haque, S. (2004). Governance and bureaucracy in Singapore: Contemporary reforms and implications, *International Political Science Review*, 25(2): 227–40.

Harvey, D. (2005). *A Brief History of Neoliberalism*. New York: Oxford University Press.

Heng, Y. K. (2012). Rajaratnam's global city vision for S'pore vindicated 40 years on. *The Straits Times*, 6 February.

Ho, H. Y. (1964/2005). The current art scene in Singapore (1960s). In *Liu, K. and H. Y. Ho. Re-Connecting: Selected Writings on Singapore Art and Art Criticism*, T. K. Sabapathy and Cheo C.-H., eds., trans. Cheo Chai-Hiang, Repr., Institute of Contemporary Arts Singapore: Singapore.

Ho, K. P. (2016). *The Ocean in a Drop: Singapore: The Next Fifty Years*. Singapore: World Scientific.

Huff, W. G. (1995). The developmental state, government, and Singapore's economic development since 1960, *World Development*, 23 (8): 1421–38.

Huxley, T. (2000). *Defending the Lion City: The Armed Forces of Singapore*. Australia: Allen & Unwin.

Inglehart, R. & Welzel, C. (2009). How development leads to democracy: what we know about modernization, *Foreign Affairs*, March/April.

Jaipragas, B. (2017). Rolling stock to laughing stock: Why is Singapore's metro struggling when Hong Kong's is a hit? *South China Morning Post*, 21 October.

Jayakumar, S. (2011). *Diplomacy: A Singapore Experience*. Singapore: Straits Times Press.

Jones, D. M. & Brown, D. (1994). Singapore and the myth of the liberalizing middle class, *The Pacific Review*, 7(1): 79–87.

Joo, Y. M. & Heng, Y. K. (2017). Turning on the taps: Singapore's new branding as a global hydrohub, *International Development Planning Review*, 39(2): 209–27.

Kathiravelu, L. (2017). Rethinking race: Beyond the CMIO categorization. In K. S. Loh, P. T. Thum, and Chia, J.M.T., eds, *Living With Myths In Singapore*. Singapore: Ethos, pp. 159–68.

Kausikan, B. (2016). Dealing with an ambiguous world. *Nathan Lectures*: I to V. Singapore.

Khamid, Hetty Musfirah Abdul. (2015). MOE to consider introducing module on race and religious issues: Heng. *Channel NewsAsia*, 8 July.

Kipnis, A. B. (2012). Constructing commonality: Standardization and modernization in Chinese nation-building, *The Journal of Asian Studies*, 71(3): 731–55.

Koh, B. S. (2017). *Brand Singapore: Nation Branding After Lee Kuan Yew, in a Divisive World*, Second Edition, e-book. Singapore: Marshall Cavendish.

Koh, T. (2016). China's perception of Singapore: 4 areas of misunderstanding. *Today*, 21 October.

Koh, T. A. (1989). Culture and the arts. In K. Sandhu & P. Wheatley, eds, *Management of Success: The Moulding of Modern Singapore*. Singapore: Institute of Southeast Asian Studies, pp. 710–48.

Koh, T. A. (2010). 'It's like rice on the table, it's our common dish': The English language and identity in Singapore. In T. Chong, ed., *Management of Success: Singapore Revisited*. Singapore: ISEAS.

Kuo, E. C. Y. (1996). Confucianism as political discourse in Singapore: the case of an incomplete revitalization movement. In Tu Weiming, ed., *Confucian Traditions in East Asian Modernity: Moral Education and Economic Culture in Japan and the Four Mini-Dragons*. Cambridge MA: Harvard University Press.

Kwa, C. G., Heng, D. T. S. & Tan, T. Y. (2009). *Singapore: A 700-Year History: From Early Emporium to World City*. National Archives of Singapore.

Kwa, J. (2016). Trust in Singapore government rises after 3-year decline: survey. *Yahoo!News*, 25 January.

Kwek, M. L. (2004). Singapore: A skyline of pragmatism. In R. Bishop, J. Philips, and W. W. Yeo, eds, *Beyond Description: Singapore Space Historicity*. London: Routledge.

Laclau, E. (1977). *Politics and Ideology in Marxist Theory: Capitalism, Fascism, Populism*. London: NLB.

Lai, A. E. (1995). *Meanings of Multiethnicity: A Case Study of Ethnicity And Ethnic Relations in Singapore*. Kuala Lumpur: Oxford University Press.

Lai, A. E. ed. (2004). *Beyond Rituals and Riots: Ethnic Pluralism and Social Cohesion in Singapore*. Singapore: Eastern Universities Press.

Lai A. E. (2017) Maze and minefield: Reflections on multiculturalism in Singapore. In Loh K. S., Thum P. T. & J. M. T. Chia, eds, *Living With Myths In Singapore*. Singapore: Ethos, pp. 169–79.

Lee, H. L. (1999). Speech at the Administrative Service Dinner and Promotion Ceremony, Singapore, 29 March.

Lee, H. L. (2000). Speech at the Singapore 21 Forum, Singapore, 16 January.

Lee, H. L. (2007). Parliamentary debate on Civil Service salary revisions, 11 April.

Lee, K. Y. (1998). Speech in parliament on the White Paper on Ministerial Salaries on 1 November 1994. In Han F. K., W. Fernandez & S. Tan, eds, *Lee Kuan Yew: The Man and His Ideas*. Singapore: Times Editions.

Lee, K. Y. (1998). *The Singapore Story: Memoirs of Lee Kuan Yew*. Singapore: Times.

Lee, K. Y. (2000). *From Third World to First: The Singapore Story: 1965–2000*. Singapore: Times.

Lee, P. (2017). New 'Passion Made Possible' campaign draws mixed reactions from netizens. *The Independent*, 25 August. www.theindependent.sg /new-passion-made-possible-campaign-draws-mixed-reactions-from-netizens/ (14 September 2017).

Lee, P. O. (2010). The four taps: water self-sufficiency in Singapore. In T. Chong, ed., *Management of Success: Singapore Revisited*. Singapore: ISEAS, pp. 417–39.

Lee, T. (2002). The politics of civil society in Singapore, *Asian Studies Review*, 26(1): 97–117.

Lee, T. (2010). *The Media, Cultural Control and Government in Singapore*. London: Routledge.

Lee, Y. N. (2015). Singapore to see largest influx of super rich. *Today*, 5 March.

Leifer, M. (2000). *Singapore's Foreign Policy: Coping With Vulnerability*. London: Routledge.

Leong, C. (2017). Pink Dot – No foreigners? No problem. *The Pride*, 19 May.

Lim, Y. L. (2017). Tianjin Eco-City a role model: Tharman. *The Straits Times*, 26 June.

Lingle, C. (1996). *Singapore's Authoritarian Capitalism, Asian Values, Free Market Illusions and Political Dependency*. Mass Market Paperback.

Liu, K. (1969/2005). Definition of an intellectual. In Liu K. *and* Ho H. Y., *Re-Connecting: Selected Writings on Singapore Art and Art Criticism*, T. K. Sabapathy & Cheo C.-H., eds., trans. Cheo C.-H., Repr., Institute of Contemporary Arts Singapore: Singapore.

Loh, K. S. (1998). Within the Singapore story: The use and narrative of history in Singapore, *Crossroads: An Interdisciplinary Journal of Southeast Asian Studies*, 12(2), 1–21.

Loh, K. S. (2013) *Squatters into Citizens: The 1961 Bukit Ho Swee Fire and the Making of Modern Singapore*. Singapore: NUS Press.

Low, L. (2001) The Singapore developmental state in the new economy and polity, *The Pacific Review*, 14(3): 411–41.

Mahbubani, K. (2009). The republic of common sense. *The Straits Times*, 9 September

McDonald, T. (2017). Is Singapore really the world's most expensive city? *BBC*, 7 April.

Medical and dental care for a small sum. (2016). *The Straits Times*, 18 December

Ministry of Community Development, Youth and Sports. (2006). Government appoints National Steering Committee on Racial and Religious Harmony, media release, 7 October.

Ministry of Manpower. (2015a). Foreign workforce numbers. www.mom.gov.sg /documents-and-publications/foreign-workforce-numbers (8 October 2017).

Ministry of Manpower. (2015b). Labour force in Singapore 2015. stats.mom .gov.sg/Pages/Labour-Force-In-Singapore-2015.aspx (8 October 2017).

Mutalib, H. (2004). *Parties and Politics: A Study of Opposition Parties and the PAP in Singapore*. Second edition. Singapore: Marshall Cavendish Academic.

NDR 2016: Singapore must choose its own place to stand on South China Sea issue, says PM Lee. (2016). *Channel NewsAsia*, 21 August.

Neo, B. S. & Chen, G. (2007). *Dynamic Governance: Embedding Culture, Capabilities and Change in Singapore*. Singapore: World Scientific.

Nye, J. S. (2013). Hard, soft, and smart power. In A.F. Cooper, J. Heine & R. Thakur, eds., *The Oxford Handbook of Modern Diplomacy*. Oxford: Oxford University Press.

Nye, J. S. (2018). How sharp power threatens soft power: the right and wrong ways to respond to authoritarian influence, *Foreign Affairs*, 24 January.

OECD. (2016). Income Inequality Update, November.

Ong, E. & Tim, M. H. (2014). Singapore's 2011 general elections and beyond: beating the PAP at its own game, *Asian Survey*, 54(4): 749–72.

Pearlman, J. (2011). Take a leaf out of S'pore story: Aussie magnate. *The Straits Times*, 16 March.

Pearson, N. (2011). Proof of welfare's multiple failings. *The Australian*, 5 March.

Peerenboom, R. (2008). *China Modernizes: Threat to the West or Model for the Rest?* Oxford: Oxford University Press.

Peh, S. H. & Goh, C. L. (2007). Life on the edge. *The Straits Times*, 7 April.

Peterson, W. (2001). *Theatre and the Politics of Culture in Contemporary Singapore*. Middletown, CT: Wesleyan University Press.

Philomin, L. E. (2014). Church must work with like-minded groups to oppose Pink Dot: Pastor. *Today*, 24 June.

Potts, J. & Cunningham, S. (2008). Four models of the creative industries, *International Journal of Cultural Policy*, 14(3): 233–47.

Parameswaran, P. (2018). What's behind Singapore's new defense budget numbers? *The Diplomat*, 22 February.

Puru Shotam, N. (1989). Language and linguistic policies. In K. S. Sandhu and P. Wheatley, eds, *Management of Success: The Moulding of Modern Singapore*, Singapore: Southeast Asian Studies, pp. 503–22.

Quah, J. (2003). *Curbing Corruption in Asia: A Comparative Study of Six Countries*. Singapore: Eastern Universities Press.

Rahim, L. Z. (1998) *The Singapore Dilemma: The Political and Educational Marginality of the Malay Community*. Kuala Lumpur: Oxford University Press.

Ramakrishna, K. (2015). *'Original Sin'?: Revising the Revisionist Critique of the 1963 Operation Coldsore in Singapore*. Singapore: ISEAS.

Raslam, K. (2016). Tharman's a perfect leader for Singapore – so what's stopping him? His ethnicity? *South China Morning Post*, 5 October.

Rodan, G. (1989). *The Political Economy of Singapore's Industrialization: National State and International Capital*. Kuala Lumpur: Forum.

Rodan, G. (2004). *Transparency and Authoritarian Rule in Southeast Asia: Singapore and Malaysia*. Oxford: Routledge.

Rodan, G. (2017). Singapore's elected president: A failed institution, *Australian Journal of International Affairs*, 12 November.

S'pore's racial harmony is 'not natural' and needs nurturing: PM Lee (2017). *Today*, 29 September.

Saadan, A. (2017). Are we working too much? Singaporeans at risk of developing health problems due to long hours. *AsiaOne*, 28 July.

Salleh, N. A. M. S & Chew, H. M. (2017). Minister Shanmugam, diplomats Bilahari and Ong Keng Yong say Prof Mahbubani's view on Singapore's foreign policy 'flawed'. *The Straits Times*, 3 July.

Segarra, L. M. (2017). These are the richest countries in the world. *Fortune*, 17 November.

Seow, B. Y. (2016). Seized SAF vehicles: APL meets HK Customs again. *The Straits Times*, 2 December.

Seow, B. Y. (2017). Singapore has the 'most powerful' passport in the world: Passport Index. *The Straits Times*, 25 October.

Seow, J. (2018). Not wise to purposely let the opposition grow bigger. *The Straits Times*, 6 April.

Siew, S. (2009). Censorship review committee. *Singapore Infopedia*, National Library Board Singapore.

Sin, C. H. (2002). The quest for a balanced ethnic mix: Singapore's ethnic quota policy examined, *Urban Studies*, 39(8): 1347–74.

Singam, C., Tan, C. K., Ng, T. & Perera, L. eds. (2002). *Building Social Space in Singapore: The Working Committee's initiative in civil society activism*. Singapore: Select Publishing.

Singapore Cultural Statistics 2016. (2016). Singapore: Ministry of Culture, Community and Youth.

Singapore Federation of Chinese Clan Associations. (1990). *Chinese Heritage*. Singapore: SFCCA.

S'pore govt loses patience with Suzhou park. (1989). *South China Morning Post*, 4 June.

Singapore riot: PM Lee Hsien Loong urges restraint. (2013). *BBC News*, 9 December.

Singapore Workforce Development Agency. (2015). Arts, design & media. www.wda.gov.sg/content/wdawebsite/L202-SingaporeJOBSpedia/L302-010B-CreativeIndustry.html (29 December 2015).

Singaporeans sleep the least – blame it on society. (2016). *The New Paper*, 8 May.

Singh, B. (2015). *Quest for Political Power: Communist Subversion and Militancy in Singapore*. Singapore: Marshall Cavendish.

Slack, J. D. (1996). The theory and method of articulation in cultural studies. In D. Morley and K.-H. Chen, eds, *Stuart Hall: Critical Dialogues in Cultural Studies*. London: Routledge.

Smartphone penetration in Singapore the highest globally: Survey. (2015). *Today*, 11 February.

Smith, C. J., Donaldson, J. A., Mudaliar, S., Md Kadir, M. & Yeoh, L. K. (2015). *A Handbook on Inequality, Poverty and Unmet Social Needs in Singapore*. Social Insight Research Series. Singapore: Lien Centre for Social Innovation.

Tan, C. (2015). It Won't Be Too Long: The Cemetery (Dawn & Dusk) by Drama Box, Singapore International Festival of Arts, Bukit Brown Cemetery, SOTA Studio Theatre/Saturday. *The Straits Times*, 20 September.

Tan, J. S. ed. (2011). *A Nation Awakes: Frontline Reflections*. Singapore: Ethos.

Tan, K. P. (2007). New politics for a renaissance city?. In K. P. Tan, ed., *Renaissance Singapore? Economy, Culture, and Politics*. Singapore: NUS Press, pp. 17–36.

Tan, K. P. (2008a). *Cinema and Television in Singapore: Resistance in One Dimension*. Leiden: Brill.

Tan, K. P. (2008b). Meritocracy and elitism in a global city: ideological shifts in Singapore, *International Political Science Review*, 29(1): 7–27.

Tan, K. P. (2009). Racial stereotypes in Singapore films: Commercial value and critical possibilities. In D. P. S. Goh, M. Gabrielpillai, P. Holden, and G. C. Khoo, eds, *Race and Multiculturalism in Malaysia and Singapore*. London: Routledge, pp. 124–40.

Tan, K. P. (2016). Choosing what to remember in neoliberal Singapore: The Singapore Story, state censorship and state-sponsored nostalgia, *Asian Studies Review*, 40(2), 231–49.

Tan, K. P. (2017) *Governing Global-City Singapore: Legacies and Futures After Lee Kuan Yew*. London: Routledge.

Tan, Y. S. (2009). *Clean, Green and Blue: Singapore's Journey Towards Environmental and Water Sustainability*. Singapore: ISEAS.

Teng, S. (2015). Curry dispute. *Singapore Infopedia*, National Library Board Singapore.

Teo, C. H. (1994). Changing worlds: political, economic and social challenges for Singapore. Speech at the SIF Singapore Student Symposium, 22 July.

Teo, Y. Y. (2018). *This is What Inequality Looks Like*. Singapore: Ethos.

Tharman Shanmugaratnam (2015). Budget speech 2015. Parliamentary speech, 23 February.

Tong, C. K. (2008). Religious trends and issues in Singapore. In Lai A. E., ed., *Religious Diversity in Singapore*. Singapore: ISEAS, pp. 28–54.

Vadaketh, S. T. & Low, D. eds. (2014). *Hard Choices: Challenging the Singapore Consensus*. Singapore: NUS Press.

Vasagar, J. (2017). Singapore-on-Thames? This is no vision for post-Brexit Britain. *The Guardian*, 24 November.

Wang, G. (2018). *Nanyang: Essays on Heritage*. Singapore: ISEAS-Yusof Ishak Institute.

Wang, K. (1998). Let's not lose National Library. *The Straits Times*, 8 December.

Weiss, M. L. (2014). Of inequality and irritation: new agendas and activism in Malaysia and Singapore, *Democratization*, 21(5): 867–87.

Which cities around the world have the highest density of millionaires? (2017). *Verdict*, 25 May.

World Bank (2018). GDP per capita (current US$). *World Bank Open Data*. https://data.worldbank.org/indicator/NY.GDP.PCAP.CD?end=2016&locations=MY-SG-Z4&start=1960 (14 June 2018).

Yao, S. (2007). *Singapore: The State and the Culture of Excess*. London: Routledge.

Yeo, G. (1991). Civic society – between the family and the state, National University of Singapore Society Inaugural Lecture, Singapore, 20 June.

Yeung, H. (2005). Institutional capacity and Singapore's developmental state: managing economic (in)security in the global economy. In Nesadurai, H. E., ed., *Globalisation and Economic Security in East Asia: Governance and Institutions*, London: Routledge.

Yong, N. (2016). Most Singaporeans would choose Tharman as the next prime minister: survey. *Yahoo!News*, 26 September.

Yue, A. (2007). Creative queer Singapore: The illiberal pragmatics of cultural production, *Gay & Lesbian Issues and Psychology Review*, 3(3): 149–58.

Zhao, L. (2009). China's S'pore Dream. *The Straits Times*, 6 February.

Zheng, Y. N. & Lim W. X. (2016). Lee Kuan Yew: the special relationship with China. In Zheng, Y. N. & Lye, L. F., eds, *Singapore-China Relations: 50 Years*. Singapore: World Scientific.

Zheng, Y. N. & Lye, L. F. (2016). Introduction. In Zheng, Y. N. and Lye, L.F., eds, *Singapore-China Relations: 50 Years*. Singapore: World Scientific.

Zuraidah Ibrahim. (2017). What Singapore is saying by expelling China hand Huang Jing. *South China Morning Post*, 12 August.

Acknowledgements

This is probably the best time to be thinking and writing about Singapore. So much uncertainty surrounds its post-Lee Kuan Yew futures. Newer discourses are emerging, taking form, gaining currency, and de-centring hitherto dominant ways of explaining the Singapore that many around the world have come to admire, but for different reasons. This Element is, in many ways, an attempt to capture the moment. It builds on the scholarship of several people I have admired and would like to thank here, such as Michael Barr, Terence Chong, Chua Beng Huat, Gillian Koh, Lai Ah Eng, Terence Lee, Loh Kah Seng, Donald Low, Kishore Mahbubani, Garry Rodan, and Carol Soon. My understanding of Singapore has also been enriched by interactions with colleagues from the Lee Kuan Yew School of Public Policy, especially Eduardo Araral, Kanti Bajpai, Chan Mun Kitt, Cheryl Chung, Suzaina Kadir, Yuen Foong Khong, Adrian Kuah, Lam Chuan Leong, Leong Ching, Dane Lim, Phua Kai Hong, Danny Quah, Ramkishen Rajan, M. Ramesh, and Yeoh Lam Keong. I also want to thank series editors Meredith L. Weiss and Edward Aspinall, who offered detailed and constructive criticisms and suggestions, all with professionalism, sensitivity, encouragement, and courteousness. Working with them was an intellectually rewarding experience. I wrote this Element with my students in mind. Since I started working at the National University of Singapore in 2001, I have taught numerous Singapore-related courses to students enrolled at its University Scholars Programme, Political Science Department, and Lee Kuan Yew School of Public Policy. It is to them that I fondly dedicate this Element.

Cambridge Elements ☰

Politics and Society in Southeast Asia

Edward Aspinall
Australian National University

Edward Aspinall is a professor of politics at the Coral Bell School
of Asia-Pacific Affairs, Australian National University. A specialist of Southeast
Asia, especially Indonesia, much of his research has focussed on democratization,
ethnic politics and civil society in Indonesia, and, most recently, clientelism
across Southeast Asia.

Meredith L. Weiss
University at Albany, SUNY

Meredith L. Weiss is Professor of Political Science at the University at Albany,
SUNY. Her research addresses political mobilization and contention,
the politics of identity and development, and electoral politics in Southeast Asia.
She is active in the American Political Science Association and Association
for Asian Studies and has held visiting fellowships or professorships
at universities in the USA, Malaysia, Singapore, the Philippines,
Japan, and Australia.

About the Series
The Elements series Politics and Society in Southeast Asia includes
both country-specific and thematic studies on one of the world's most dynamic
regions. Each title, written by a leading scholar of that country or theme,
combines a succinct, comprehensive, up-to-date overview of debates
in the scholarly literature with original analysis and a clear argument.

Cambridge Elements $\equiv$

Politics and Society in Southeast Asia

Elements in the Series